# IFOR
## on
# IFOR

*This book*
*is dedicated*
*to Alina*

# IFOR o

# n IFOR

# NATO PEACEKEEPERS IN BOSNIA-HERZEGOVINA

Edited by Rupert Wolfe Murray
Photographs by Steven Gordon
Foreword by Richard Holbrooke

# MAP OF BOSNIA-HERZEGOVINA

## Showing the Entity Boundary Line and IFOR Divisional Boundaries

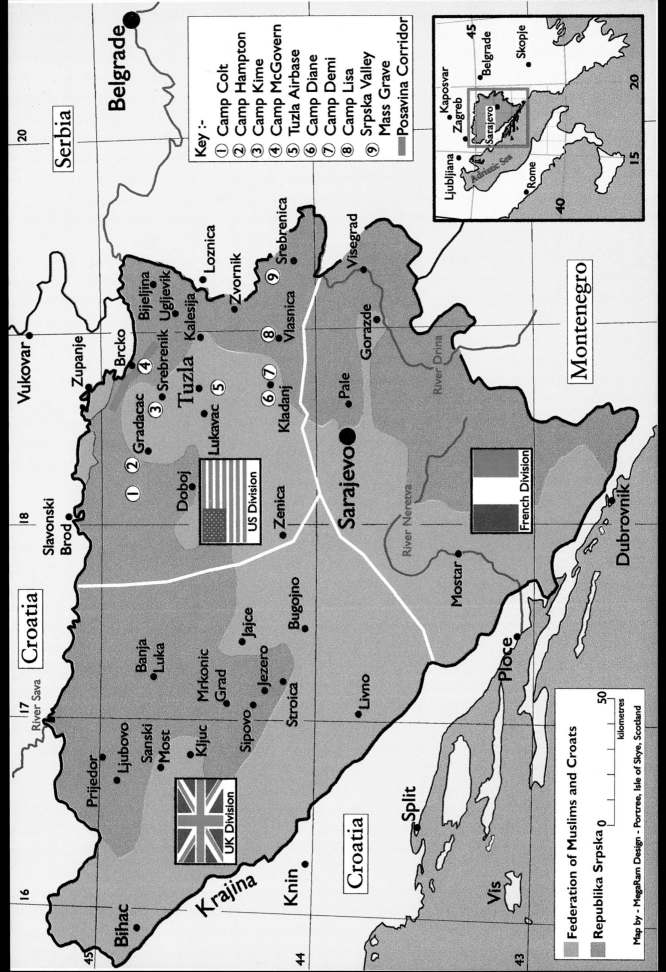

Key:-
① Camp Colt
② Camp Hampton
③ Camp Kime
④ Camp McGovern
⑤ Tuzla Airbase
⑥ Camp Diane
⑦ Camp Demi
⑧ Camp Lisa
⑨ Srpska Valley
◆ Mass Grave
▬ Posavina Corridor

US Division

French Division

UK Division

Federation of Muslims and Croats

Republika Srpska

0                    50
kilometres

Map by - MegaRam Design - Portree, Isle of Skye, Scotland

# CONTENTS

**IFOR on IFOR**

Title page.
Kaposvar, Hungary:
lines of US Army 'Humvee'
jeeps wait in line to go to
Bosnia with Military
Police units.

# FOREWORD
## *Richard Holbrooke*

The idea of a book on IFOR (NATO's Implementation Force in Bosnia) is a timely one. These pages bring together the personnel of many armies, some of whom have not always been friendly to one another. In Bosnia-Herzegovina these forces have been able to co-exist and work together extraordinarily well.

There has been no war for nearly a year in Bosnia. This is not a real peace, but as a result of the Dayton Agreements and the work of IFOR, thousands of people are alive today who might otherwise be dead or wounded. The rebuilding of this war-torn country has begun. Without IFOR this could not have happened.

The title *IFOR on IFOR* is most appropriate: it is the people working for IFOR who do the talking – with such spontaneity that this book brings the whole vast exercise to life. We find the Russian Commander, British gunners, Romanian engineers, a French chef, an Italian priest, Bosnian, Serbian and Croatian translators; Malaysians, Norwegians, Turks and Canadians, and of course the Americans.

*IFOR on IFOR* gives a unique insight into IFOR's role in a country whose recent turmoil has gripped the world. This is not a book about war, it is a book about people and peace-keeping. Having played a role in the events leading to IFOR's creation, I am honored to introduce this book to what I hope will be a wide audience.

RICHARD HOLBROOKE

New York

*August, 1996*

Richard Holbrooke
in September 1994, at
Gornji Vakuf, central Bosnia.

Photograph © Paul Harris

# INTRODUCTION
## *Rupert Wolfe Murray*

The idea for this book came about when we discovered that American troops based in Tuzla had an enormous appetite for the book *Cry Bosnia*. In fact, this book of war photographs by Paul Harris became a best-seller in the network of PX shops throughout the American Division. The idea of a second book of photographs, this time specifically focused on the peace-keepers rather than on Bosnia itself, sprang immediately to mind.

I arrived in Tuzla in January 1996, about a month after the American Division of IFOR set up their headquarters in Tuzla's military airbase. I had come to Bosnia with a very different agenda – to research a humanitarian aid project for a new Scottish aid agency called Connect. This involved making a couple of quick visits to Mostar and writing a report, but Bosnian friends in Tuzla made me feel so welcome that I decided to stay on.

For a while I worked as a volunteer editor in Mayor Beslagic's office in Tuzla, editing his English language communiqués for the outside world. This was an inspirational time as Beslagic is well-known the world over as a tolerant and charismatic leader, credited for holding together the delicate ethnic balance in Tuzla while it collapsed elsewhere in the country with disastrous results.

> The people we help are handicapped, often as a direct result of the war; we supply them with equipment or funds to open small businesses, giving them a foundation on which they can start building their future.

During that time President Clinton invited Mayor Beslagic to the 'National Prayer Breakfast' in Washington DC, a ceremonial event for world figures that takes place every year. The reports came back that the Americans were impressed that Beslagic did not complain or blame other ethnic groups, rather he addressed the concrete problems Tuzla and its people were facing. My opinion of Bosnian political practices was formed during that time and it was a cruel shock to learn that many areas of Bosnia are profoundly undemocratic.

During this time I had no contact with the huge American force of twenty thousand troops that was building up in the area. The total number of IFOR troops in Bosnia was agreed at sixty thousand. I was living in Tuzla, trying to learn the language and getting to know the people and there was this huge number of Americans nearby whom we could never meet. In fact trying to meet an American soldier in Bosnia is a mission in itself. They are not allowed to leave camp unless on patrol: armed, flakjacketed, helmeted and accompanied by a platoon. They are certainly not allowed to have a drink or fraternise with the locals. At first I thought these rules were ridiculous but I must confess I gradually began to respect the way the Americans went about things.

Contact first came when I tried to sell copies of *Cry Bosnia* to the PX shop in Tuzla airbase. The first American IFOR member I met was John McGhee, a charismatic AAFES manager, and his enthusiasm for *Cry Bosnia* and everything we were trying to do knew no bounds. It also seemed that the demand for *Cry Bosnia*, among Americans as well as the other NATO personnel who frequented the airbase, knew no limit. In a small way we

Detailed view of the tracks and wheels of US Army 'Panther' de-mining tank (as seen on cover).

provided the IFOR troops, particularly the Americans, with an insight, a snapshot, into Bosnia and its recent bloody history.

For Connect these book sales were hugely important because they provided us with enough money to set up a humanitarian agency in Mostar and support Income Generating Projects in Sarajevo, Zenica and Tuzla. Many of the people we help are handicapped, often as a direct result of the war; we supply them with equipment or funds to open small businesses, giving them a foundation on which they can start building their future. The profits from *IFOR on IFOR* will go towards these projects so all those who buy a copy will be involved in a small way.

When we decided to go ahead with this book it was difficult to know where to begin, who to approach, and how to get the people that mattered to take us seriously. It was slow at first, hard to break through that thick defensive wall of army bureaucracy. But then we came across General Nash who was visiting the Russian IFOR base near Bijeljina. Nash spotted me from twenty paces away and scrutinised me as if to say, 'Who the hell is this guy?' Then he saw I was clutching a copy of *Cry Bosnia* and he said, 'We sell that book in our PX shops'. Before I was hurried away by his staff, I told him we were planning a new book and he nodded and said, 'Yeah. Contact my Chief of Staff'.

> My technique was simple.
> I would ask my subjects the
> same set of questions:
> What can you tell me about your
> background?
> Why and how did you join the army?
> What are your experiences in the army?
> What have you done in Bosnia?
> What do you think of IFOR in Bosnia?

From that moment on it was all go – the doors started to open, we found ourselves welcome guests all over the American Divisional area; the British took us in, the French, Turkish and Swedish Commanders gave us on the spot interviews, things started to happen. Paul Harris lent us his Skoda car, an old war-horse that sped us all over the country without breaking under the stress of the most appalling roads in Europe. In the three months it took us to cover all of Bosnia-Herzegovina, meeting the armies and collecting the material, a ten thousand kilometre journey, we only spent six nights in hotels or guest houses. This saved us valuable funds and allowed us to meet some of the colourful characters who inhabit every military establishment.

The initial idea had been to do a photographic book on the IFOR troops, their equipment and their work. Steven Gordon, a young photographer from Glasgow, abandoned a job he was doing on the drugs scene in the wake of the cult film *Trainspotting*, and came out to do the photographs. My role was simply to write some text, the bare minimum, to go alongside the pictures.

But then the characters in IFOR took over and the text started to assume a life of its own. I started interviewing IFOR personnel so I could have some raw material for the 'filler' text, but I found the opinions, backgrounds and experiences of the soldiers so interesting and unique in their own right that I put these voices centre-stage and allowed them to speak for themselves. My technique was simple. I would ask my subjects the same set of questions: What can you tell me about your background? Why and how did you join the army? What are your experiences in the army? What have you done in Bosnia? What do you think of IFOR in Bosnia? These questions were enough to open a whole world of individual experiences and views. I would record their voices on tape, transcribe them to paper, editing out my own questions.

I was going to write an introduction that included a short history of Bosnia and explain

how the people of this country are victims of the rabid nationalism that started in Serbia and spread to Croatia. I wanted to put my own views into this book because here was an opportunity to write on an issue about which I feel strongly. But I came to realise that this is not the place for my views. There are plenty of books that put forward the Bosnians' case, the most comprehensive of which is *BOSNIA: A Short History* by Noel Malcolm (New York University Press in USA, Macmillan in UK). If anyone wants to learn about Bosnia they should read this book and study the bibliography for references to other objective books on the subject. My role was to talk to the soldiers, cooks, commanders and translators who make up IFOR and get their words onto paper.

Although I don't agree with all the views expressed here, in fact some of them I find quite shocking, these are the genuine opinions of some IFOR personnel and it would be wrong to disguise or 'prettify' what the soldiers feel. Above all, I see this book as an opportunity for the people in IFOR to express themselves. I was simply the medium, the tool, through which their words were transcribed onto the printed page.

There are many people without whom the making of this book would not have been possible; Stephanie, my mother, for continual support and encouragement; Paul Harris for help on many fronts; Jasminko Arnautovic for persuading me to stay in Tuzla during 1996; the British Press Officers; Chris Stephen for interviewing the French and Italians; Andy Tilly and Annabelle and Toby Gough in the UK; John McGhee and all those enthusiastic folk at AAFES. There are a score of people who made it happen in the US sector: Colonel Brzozowski, Sergeant Glynn, Major Suttle and Colonel Briscoe. But the people who deserve most thanks for this book are those who are interviewed here.

## PART 1

IFOR
on
IFOR

# The US Division

# THE AMERICAN HQ

## William Nash

MAJOR GENERAL
COMMANDER OF AMERICAN DIVISION 'TASK FORCE EAGLE'

**Interviewed at Tuzla Airbase**

"When I finished High School I rebelled against the Army and went off to a civilian college for two and a half years and disavowed any intention of joining the Army. Why? The ignorance of youth I suppose. I had known very little except the Army as I grew up. It was the era of the Beatniks – we weren't hippies in those days, this was a long time ago, the very early sixties and I just wanted to go off and do my own thing, not have all that regimentation.

So I ended up going to college in the south, in New Orleans, a Chemistry Major of all things. It wasn't for two and a half years that I realised my life's path went through an army post. I wasn't sure at first if I was running away or running towards something. I did in fact have a focus on my life's work so I quit college and joined the Army as a private.

What makes a good soldier? Dedication to service, a willingness to put his personal needs behind those of his unit and his nation. I really enjoyed it, in fact I was having so much fun that had it not been for my mother I probably would never have become an officer. She literally filled out the application to the Military Academy and sent it to me to sign.

> I learned some very valuable soldierly lessons in Vietnam: the importance of discipline, the importance of proper military behaviour in the conduct of military operations. I learned about dealing with people and how it was to lead folks.

It was an Army of transition at that time. We were going from the folks that had served in World War Two but were retiring, to the new army that was about to enter Vietnam. It was the era of McNamara and the revolution in the management of the armed forces. There were some very great soldiers in that time but there was an overall misunderstanding within the nation of what Vietnam was all about. I learned some very valuable soldierly lessons in Vietnam: the importance of discipline, the importance of proper military behaviour in the conduct of military operations. I learned about dealing with people and how it was to lead folks.

I think a lot of us were deeply affected by our experience in Vietnam and wanted to make an Army that would not be the kind of Army we became in Vietnam: out of focus and not based on the foundations of discipline, training and dedication. Not to criticise but to realise the foundations of our profession and meet the highest standards.

We've learned to look at each other and to look at ourselves and to analyse and to study and to be willing to acknowledge mistakes and correct them. Some would say that during the earlier period we would tend to overlook, hide or ignore mistakes or lessons and now it's a very concentrated effort to learn from everything we do. We have a very large programme in the army, both formal and informal, that focuses on the learning process.

Previous pages.
US Army 1st Brigade engineers at Camp McGovern near Brcko.

Opposite page, top.
Major General Nash, Commander of Task Force Eagle, visits troops in Camp Colt, near Gradacac.

Bottom.
Major General Nash inspects the crew of an M1A1 Abrams Main Battle Tank at Camp Colt.

Even though we're fully engaged here we take the time to get smarter every day. It's not the generals who have got to get smarter, although they certainly do, but it's the sergeants and privates and lieutenants and captains who have the ideas on how to do things, ideas that you have to integrate into your process. As a group, today's Army is a better army and the soldiers are better soldiers, more physically fit, more dedicated. The soldiers today are volunteers, they have come to serve their nation. They're smart, God they're smart, they're committed and they work hard to be good. They go beyond the Spartan ideal because in addition to being stoic they are also smart, and so they can figure out how to get things done really well.

It's hard being away from your families, it's hard not being able to 'chill' as the soldiers would say, but it's part of the business and I think the vast majority of the soldiers fully understand and support our methods of operation and force protection measures here.

A lot of lieutenants start out wanting to be generals but, the older you get and the smarter you get, you realise that it's a pretty hard job so you better be careful what you pray for. What matters most is service and giving your best and there are a lot of good people that don't end up being generals. The greatest soldier I knew was never a general – my father. He died as a colonel. He was a great soldier and I don't think I could fill his boots at all.

From my foxhole it's going well. Ultimately peace in Bosnia-Herzegovina is the responsibility of the people and their leaders. The international community has decided to intervene in a very strong and positive way to assist that effort because there appears to be a general desire from the people and leaders of Bosnia-Herzegovina to achieve peace – despite a wide variety of problems. The NATO Forces, IFOR, were organised, equipped and designed to achieve the military portion of the solution to long-term peace. We entered the country in December '95 and, with the co-operation of the former warring factions, went about implementing the military provisions of the Dayton Accord. All four armies have done their job pretty well in achieving the objectives set out in Annex 1A of the Dayton Accord. But I don't know if the military aspects bring peace as much as they bring the absence of war.

Given that condition – the absence of war – in a reasonably secure environment, it's certainly not perfect, certainly not eliminated the criminal activity, and there is certainly a potential for some terrorist activity, but the conventional military aspects are in very good shape. The armies are back in the barracks, the vehicles are lined up in the cantonment areas, the air defence guns are put away. The only army running around Bosnia-Herzegovina at the moment is IFOR, and that's pretty good.

But it's the political, social and economic aspects that must rise to the top and that's where the international community and the people and leaders of Bosnia-Herzegovina need to focus in order to achieve long-term peace and stability. We could stay ten years and if they don't want peace there's going to be another war. What was very pleasing to us was the degree of co-operation we got from the very beginning – from the military forces, the factions. That surprised us and we had to adapt to that attitude very quickly. We expected more obstinacy on the part of all parties, much more so than was ever displayed.

It's really the culmination of a life's work to come together on this large scale operation in the cause of peace as opposed to World War Three. One of the great things about this operation – and a very important strategic dimension – is the NATO role in European security after the Cold War. It's been a great opportunity to have Multi-National Division North, Task Force Eagle, come together with the NATO allies, along with the partnership for peace forces that have come about since the Cold War ended.

American Black Hawk helicopter takes off in front of the Russian Brigade HQ, located by Ugljevik power station, near Bijeljina.
Note the Apache helicopter in the background, these accompany Black Hawks as armed escorts when high ranking officers are flying. General Nash was inside the Black Hawk pictured here.

So we have Polish units, Swedish units, Finnish units, as part of the division; it's very, very special. The Turks, NATO soldiers, then you come to the Russians – gosh, what a wonderful thing for Europe, for the world, that the United States and Russia were able to come together and make an agreement to co-operate and co-ordinate their military activities in the cause of peace. I'm as impressed with the Russian forces as I expected to be. I think their commander's a professional – dedicated, capable, and it's been a pleasure both personally and professionally to work with the Russian forces.

General Alexander Lentsov, Sasha, will be a life-long friend. The behind-the-scenes story I will share with you would be about the first morning we had a conference call. Now Sasha doesn't speak too much English but he speaks a little. We began the conference call where I have all the Brigade Commanders in all the sectors in the division area on the telephone with me in my command centre and it's on a speaker so my staff can hear. The first day that he came on the telephone and I said 'Russian Brigade', that meant it was his time to report and the first words out of his mouth were 'Good morning my commander'. A chill went up my spine, that I had a Russian commander speaking to me like that.

He has consistently performed to the highest professional standards, co-operated thoroughly. When we had views, as Divisional Commanders and Brigade Commanders always have, that differ, we talk them out as a Divisional Commander and a Brigade Commander talk them out without regard to nationality. On the ground the strategic issues have converged and therefore operationally and tactically we are one. We leave it to our superiors to hammer out the strategic issues. We're got a job to do and we're clear on the job so we go about getting it done.

To serve with all the soldiers in Multi-National Division North is a great honour and privilege. For the American soldier I would just as soon have you for a son or a daughter than I would for a soldier. They're great people, they're hard working, they're committed to doing their damnedest to achieving peace in Bosnia."

# Vlad Petnicki

CAPTAIN, USAF

**Interviewed at Tuzla air base**

"It's a bizarre story but not from the Balkan standpoint. My mother's side had come from a long line of wealthy families: politicians, diplomats, vineyard owners. After the Second World War they lost all that because of the Communists.

My father is called Zvonimir Petnicki, which means the tolling of peace. He was born in Croatia, Zagreb, in 1907 – a two generation gap between father and son. My father's father was a postal official in the Austro-Hungarian Empire. They moved quite a bit and probably because of that he learned so many languages. They moved to Bratislava, to Budapest and then back into Croatia, all within the empire's postal system. My father learned Serbo-Croatian, Hungarian, French, Italian, English, Russian and German. German was probably his weakest, but I give him credit for language number seven.

After the First World War, when the Austro-Hungarian Empire broke up, they moved into the Kingdom of Serbs, Croats and Slovenes. My father went to school in Dijon, France, and his father wanted him to study economics but he found it very boring and after a year switched to ancient history, but he didn't tell his father for another year.

Top.
A Russian media officer photographs an American Apache AH64 Attack helicopter.

Bottom.
Detailed view of the weapon system on an Apache AH64 Attack helicopter. The Hellfire laser guided missiles on the left cost $40,000 each and are capable of bursting open the strongest tanks. The pod on the right can launch various types of rockets with deadly accuracy up to 9 kilometres.

He came back to Yugoslavia in the 1930s and became a high school teacher in Split. He taught French and ancient history. In 1941 Yugoslavia was invaded by Germany and her allies and after being subdued in less than two weeks it was divided up. The Croatians got their own puppet state, Italy got Dalmatia and Croatia took Bosnia, I guess partly as recompense for losing the Dalmatian coast. Serbia was placed under direct German control.

My father, being in Split, was not in a pinch yet because the Italians were fairly mild compared to their Teutonic allies. He spent six months in an Italian prison camp and I don't know exactly the reason why, although we can assume it was for activities in support of the Resistance and against the Occupation.

By 1943 Italy was falling out of the war. This was the time my father was in an Italian jail and it was there that he learned the language. He talked his way out of prison about a week before the Ustache came down and took over from the Italians, who were retreating. As the Italians were pulling out, the Camp Commander changed and my father, by now fluent in Italian, made a great deal of his innocence and the innocence of his fellow prisoners, that this was all a big misunderstanding. For whatever reason, the guy believed him, or the guy just had a merciful heart, and they were released a couple of weeks before certain death at the hands of the Ustache.

> My father would say, "Tito – I can't say anything bad about him. He was good to me."  I think he also believed in what Tito was trying to do in terms of keeping Yugoslavia together and dissolving the nationalistic visions into this new "Brotherhood and Unity".

At that point there was nothing for them to do but go into the hills. In the early years of the Partisan Movement the majority of the Partisans, a huge majority, were Serbs from Bosnia, and all the areas where the Ustache had started their exterminations. They took to the hills because they had no choice. 1943 saw the biggest entry of Croatians into the Partisans – from Dalmatia. My father was in that group. He managed to hook up with the Partisans and with Tito. He became the Liaison Officer for Sir Fitzroy Maclean who was parachuted into Yugoslavia by Churchill to figure out who was doing the best job of fighting the Germans and establish that liaison between the British and Tito. Based on those reports, the British threw in their lot behind Tito and abandoned Mihailovic's Chetniks. He was the British and American liaison officer until the end of the war.

My father was in Drvar when the Germans made their last attempt to get Tito on the 25th of May, 1944. They parachuted airborne troops in there in an attempt to catch Tito and they nearly did – he was wounded. My dad was a little bit further away but he obviously had to hightail it out of there as well. After that, the British had to move the whole headquarters to the island of Vis and then they didn't have so many problems because the Germans couldn't reach them there.

My father would say, "Tito – I can't say anything bad about him. He was good to me". I think he also believed in what Tito was trying to do in terms of keeping Yugoslavia together and dissolving the nationalistic visions into this new "Brotherhood and Unity". It was a noble fight. He was one of the people, one of the unfortunately too few people, who always in the census listed their nationality as Yugoslav. Unfortunately, that was probably no more than ten or twelve per cent, if it was that much. Maybe it was the wrong basis on which to try to unite the diverse peoples of Yugoslavia.

In the post-war period my father became Tito's chief interpreter. He travelled everywhere Tito went, since French and English were basically the languages of currency pretty much used everywhere you went, especially in Africa and Asia. He became chief

Top.
US Army troops disembark from C-130 Hercules transport plane in Hungary on R&R leave from Bosnia.

Bottom.
Vlad Petnicki, a captain in the United States Air Force, stands by the flightline at Tuzla airbase. Captain Petnicki is the official interpreter to General Nash and his father was the interpreter for President Tito.

interpreter of the Yugoslav Foreign Ministry and kept that position from 1946 through 1972. In 1972 he went to New York and became chief interpreter to the United Nations mission. He pointed out to me when I was young that this was really taking a lower job but my mother and he decided to do this because they wanted me to learn English. Of course, I wound up staying in the United States, so it was a really fateful decision.

My father is a very private man. He is from the old school – very formal and very distant, not in terms of expressing personal affection but in terms of expressing his deepest feelings, thoughts or philosophies. He always helped anybody who came across his way and did his job and didn't dabble in politics.

1976 is when the American bicentenary happened and it was also an American election year. I got very caught up following both events in a naive, sheltered sort of way, and I was a very naive, sheltered child which is typical of children brought up in this part of the world.

Around that time I started developing a split personality. I started rebelling against going back to Yugoslavia but once I was back with my friends and grandparents by the sea, on the Adriatic . . . I still think of those summers as the greatest time of my life. After 1977 the American side started winning. My teenage rebellion was not drugs or illicit sex, it was against my roots and after the summer of 1977, I basically became old enough for my parents to accept that I was not going back. I didn't want anything to do with Communism. My father retired in 1981 and my parents returned to Yugoslavia. I stayed.

I grew up in a very liberal part of New York City and I considered myself a liberal. But the one thing I was never liberal on was the Communist thing. I was always a down-the-line right-winger, I guess because I'd seen it with my own eyes. The last few years that I came to Yugoslavia when I was fifteen and sixteen, for the summers, I started seeing things like very crude censorship of television that was really kind of comical at times. It offended me although I can't say that it persecuted me.

> In 1989 Communism changed and all of a sudden we saw that the world order was not permanently fixed in the way it had been for 45 years.

I graduated from Law School in 1986 and my parents would visit for two or three months of every year. I worked for about two years as an attorney in a small law firm – not what I wanted to do. Then I worked for a couple of very large insurance firms. Something was missing and I hated those six years in New Jersey, commuting to and from work.

I was not happy with my legal career. When I was younger my mother always wanted me to be a journalist because you could travel a lot but, probably because it was what my mother said, I wanted the opposite. It was starting to bore me out of my mind. In 1991, during the Gulf War, the idea came into my mind to look into going into the military as a Judge Advocate because I was grinding my teeth watching CNN, wishing I were part of it. I had always thought my father had had an interesting life and has lived through such a great war and what a great adventure and now – nothing. Well, 1989 was no longer nothing. In 1989 Communism changed and all of a sudden we saw that the world order was not permanently fixed in the way it had been for forty five years.

I announced to my parents that when I got my US citizenship I was going to join the military. My mother didn't think it was a great idea, she thought I was doing OK in my legal career. In 1991 I applied for and got a commission as a Judge Advocate in the United States Air Force (USAF).

By that stage the war in former Yugoslavia had already begun. My parents had to return

A burnt out Serbian T-55 tank in a village near Orasije, just south of the Sava river. The Soviet and Yugoslav built tanks that were extensively used by the Bosnian Serb Army are outdated and vulnerable to attack from readily available RPG-7s (Rocket Propelled Grenades) and other shoulder fired, tank busting weapons.

to Belgrade because that was where they had retired from and the currencies could no longer cross borders. They wanted to return to Croatia and not go back to Milosevic's Belgrade. My father doesn't discuss politics but my mother's not like that, she's a typical Serb: very highly strung, opinionated, somewhat paranoid and doggedly, bulldog determined and I've inherited that from her. One of the things she told me this May when she could speak a little more freely about what she had seen in the last five years was, 'in my 65 years I never dreamed that I would be ashamed to say that I am a Serb, but because of Milosevic I now am ashamed'. I think that tells you enough about my parents' views about the current situation.

I hope I never practice law for another day as a civilian again. I wanted to wear the uniform. You cannot be a male raised in the Balkans and steeped in the tradition of the Balkans and not love the military. Frankly, that's why I think the war caught on so quickly because it had been glamourised so much through the history of struggle and guerrilla warfare, going back to the Illyrians. I knew that I would fit into military life and I knew that I did not fit into civilian life because I was just a little bit too disciplined, a little bit too clear on what's right and what's wrong than most Americans. I spent most of my life trying to become an American, it took me nineteen and a half years to get my citizenship. Culturally, I stopped speaking the Serbo-Croatian language.

I didn't go back after 1977 to even visit, didn't associate with any émigrés because the émigrés in the US, both the Serb and Croatian ones, in the vast majority bring their politics back with them. I don't hate anybody based on their ethnicity and being half, ethnically speaking, Croatian and half Serb, I can't afford to. I think most people in the former Yugoslavia feel the same way but people are very gullible and as one of the locals here told me the people of the Balkans are very quick to respond to the call of the war drum.

I thought I was all-American, but when I got to about thirty I started realising how different I was; my background and what I'd seen myself gave me a completely different view of life and I realised in a very fundamental way I was not, and never would be, a hundred per cent part of the American home-grown culture. There was a part of me that, as much as I tried to forget it, I could not. There is a cultural, tribal bond here that doesn't exist in America, so I'm kind of split between two places. You can try and spit on your past and forget it but guess what? It's still there and it fundamentally affects you.

By then I realised forgetting my language was kind of dumb and I started relearning Serbo-Croat. The one thing that took real study was military, technical and legal terminology. The rest of the stuff was there and I was amazed at how quickly the cobwebs got cleared. I started taking the annual Foreign Language Proficiency Test, which is the Department of Defence exam. Once you take it, it identifies you as that speaker and from then on you can't hide, and I didn't want to hide. For three years I told my chain of command I'm here, volunteering for any kind of Bosnia mission, frankly thinking in terms of advancing my career, by making myself a little different from everybody else, rather than any desire to come back.

By August '95 I became the top rated Serbo-Croatian linguist in the USAF. If you can imagine I had my fishing pole in the water for three years, suddenly there were bites. In October, I was out on exercise at an army base and in the middle of the exercise the Wing Commander came to visit everybody and he took me aside and said, 'Hey, we've got a call, they're going to send you to Dayton'. I was overwhelmed with dual emotions: absolute fear and absolute exhilaration at a great opportunity.

I went to Dayton as an Assistant Liaison Officer with tremendously mixed emotions.

An HVO (Bosnian Croat Army) engineer scans a suspected minefield for unexploded ordnance, there are tens of millions of landmines scattered all over Bosnia and it will take decades to remove them all.

We were not assigned to any particular delegation but which ever one of the three Liaison Officers needed us we would go with them. For the first week we worked with all three delegations. Then I realised if I'm running around helping three delegations I'm not doing much good. Better to be focused than being a glorified waiter. The other guys felt the same.

The Yugoslav delegation, with Milosevic in it, was the first to fly in on a plane that was referred to as 'the flying bar' because they brought so much liquor with them that they were giving it away from the first night. I met a couple of guys who had worked with my dad and of course they had warm feelings and good things to say about him. I did not want to work for the Serbian delegation and when I saw them when they first came in, Milosevic and all the other high ranking guys, I looked at them and instantly one thought went through my mind, 'this is the exact same scum that I ran away from twenty years ago'.

The Bosnians, to me, were the party that had suffered the most but there was no great desire for me to work with the Bosnians. I knew the Serbs and I knew the Croats but the Bosnians were an unknown entity, as they still are to a large extent. The Croatians are something else. My father is Croatian and I spent the best summers of my life in Croatia. The one thing you could see when the Croatians came in was that they didn't need any interpreters. Most of their people knew four or five languages. On the street you wouldn't be able to tell them from an average American. Half their delegation had been émigrés. Very smooth, very polished people, people I felt a kinship with not only at a cultural level but on a Western level. They were easy to work with and were falling over themselves to be pro-western, to be friendly. I personally think that for all the stuff that may or may not be going on there, Croatia will eventually be pulled towards the West, perhaps against itself because there are some other forces pulling in the other direction.

> Milosevic and all the other high ranking guys, I looked at them and instantly one thought went through my mind, "this is the exact same scum that I ran away from twenty years ago".

So I ended up being an Assistant Liaison Officer for the Croatian delegation. We were there at all hours making sure all their whims were catered for, making sure that everything ran smoothly in terms of security. All the presidents brought their own security and there was State Department security and Secret Service and the Air Force Office of Special Investigations (OSI) – an awful lot of people with a little wire running out of their ears going over the place. It was absolutely confusing for everybody because nobody had been there before.

The war had lasted so long, the three sides were bled dry and every one of them needed to have the war end. Every one of them couldn't end the war on their own for political reasons back home. Having whipped up nationalist sentiment you cannot then say, 'Hey, maybe we should stop without achieving everything'. They needed to have somebody to knock their heads together so they could say, 'Hey, they made us do it'. And that somebody was Holbrooke and the US. The Europeans had no credibility.

Ultimately what comes out of this, the best that is going to happen, is that Bosnia is Lebanised. It's going to be a country that exists on paper but, in reality, it's going to be controlled by different outside powers. That's basically what happened. You had President Tudjman of Croatia and President Milosevic of Serbia, something that the locals here like to throw up at us, who came in and made decisions and signed agreements covering about two thirds of Bosnia, but they are not Bosnians. That gives you a pretty good idea of what

Russian troops unloading rocks into the vehicle park at the Russian Brigade HQ, located by Ugljevik power station.

went on.

I remember setting up a luncheon at the Officers' Club for Milosevic and Tudjman. It turned out to be a five hour luncheon. Beforehand, they had a cocktail and I was one of the flies on the wall alongside all the Secret Service people. I had a clear view of Milosevic and the thing that struck me immediately was how smooth this guy was, he reminded me of a used car salesman or a good ol' boy. He called President Tudjman by his first name, Franjo, which I thought was real tacky.

He launched into this 'Well, Franjo, we can resolve all this. This whole thing was a mistake and it shouldn't have happened . . . we need to end this thing . . . we need to get our economies integrated and working again. . .we've got a chance to do everything here, we've got a chance to solve everything right here . . .' He was going on and on in this fashion. Tudjman is a very proper old school conservative gentleman so he doesn't betray his emotions. He just stood there looking very severe, sometimes nodding his head, sometimes shaking it. At one point I remember Milosevic saying, 'But of course we have to have an outlet to the Adriatic'. And you could see Tudjman shaking his head severely and Milosevic said, 'Well, come on, you have five hundred kilometres of coastline, you can give us a couple'. I imagine it was more of the same kind of thing behind closed doors.

The agreement came together during the last hour and a half, literally while everybody was preparing to leave unsuccessfully. Then everyone was breaking their necks to make the final ceremony and then the aeroplane flights. One of my friends, an OSI officer from my base, was the bodyguard for Sacirbey, the Bosnian Foreign Minister. He had a very uncomfortable moment that last night when everybody stayed up the whole night.

He was in a room with Holbrooke and Sacirbey and they were having a shouting match. Sacirbey was going on how 'We can't accept that map, we can't accept that map'. And Holbrooke said, 'Look, we've been here for three and a half weeks. This is all you're going to get.' And I think that's kind of the way it happened. Nobody was happy with the final outcome but the peace was signed because all three sides had to take a break, they had painted themselves into a corner and they needed somebody else, like the US, to get them out.

Holbrooke is obviously a very brilliant man, he's not a Wall Street trader for nothing. He's got what I would call the typical New Yorker personality; he's very 'in your face', he's very aggressive and he doesn't let these guys get away with anything – which is what all the other clowns from Europe were doing for four and a half years. They were letting themselves be boxed into signing these meaningless ceasefires. Holbrooke put their feet to the fire and he didn't take any of their crap. I think they saw he would back up what he was saying, that there would be consequences. I think he is the only one who put them in a defensive position. As a character, he's a man very aware of his presence. When Holbrooke walks into a room he's looking around. It's clear he's announcing his presence. When he walks into a room you know he's there. He's kind of a showman and very much a domineering personality which is what these guys needed because that's the only thing they understand. Holbrooke is the guy who put this whole thing together and got us here, his personality made the difference.

Inevitably I was called up to go to Bosnia. The first thing I did when I got here, on February 1, was go and investigate the death of Sergeant Dugan, the American who was killed in the mine blast. The general said I was to use both my skills, linguistic and legal, on this job.

General Nash has a day to day interpreter, he flies with him everywhere, whereas I am his interpreter at all the official meetings. At this point, the parallel with my father's career

was starting to hit me. My father said a translator should only be translating into his strongest language, which for me is English. I could do as good a job of translating Serbo-Croat into English as anybody, well, almost anybody they can find out there – but given that Serbo-Croat was no longer my strongest language it was quite challenging and nerve-wracking. But I did well and everyone complimented me. I learned quickly on the job.

By the first Joint Military Commission meeting I was ready. If you can imagine it. A huge tent with maybe seventy or eighty people sitting in the audience and a table in the front with nine generals sitting around it – and I am the sole interpreter. The thing that the general liked was that I was not a shrinking violet. At one of the meetings earlier the general had said that he wanted me to project more and act like him. I always thought the interpreters were supposed to be in the background and inconspicuous. He wanted me to be demonstrative: he bangs his fist, I bang my fist. At the next meeting when he banged his fist to make a point, I banged my fist harder. I later heard he got a kick out of that.

My legal training has probably been the most important thing. I don't have any fear of talking in front of people because I had conquered that fear right after law school when it was quite substantial. That, plus the ability to project my voice, is really what differentiates me from just about all the other interpreters we have here.

General Nash is a very persuasive speaker. He has the ability to befriend people. He's a man's man and that's what those guys respond to. At the beginning the emphasis was on establishing personal relationships with these guys. With the Bosnians and Croats it wasn't such a big deal because they were trying so hard to be our friends. With the Serbs it was very tense at first, there was a lot of anxiety on their side. But as they saw that we weren't coming on one side against the other, and that General Nash has shown that he is here as an independent honest broker, you could see the relationship changing as the meetings went on.

Now all three sides consider him to be a friend because he has repeatedly shown, through his actions, his goodwill and good intentions. No shots have been fired and I think that is in large measure due to the calm, patience and level headedness of our commander. He has a way of motivating the soldiers, of patting them on the back in a very expressive way. Just saying a little thing will keep somebody flying high and feeling good for a week. He also challenges soldiers and expects nothing but the best – and he usually gets it.

I'll say the same thing my father said about Tito – and don't compare him to Tito – is that he's been very good to me. You know what's expected if you're working for him and you know you'd better bust your butt to do the job, and do it right, because you don't want to be on the receiving end of even one of his mild blue lightning bolts – as they are called in the nightly briefings. Nash is a great leader, he relates well to his troops, he's a tremendous motivator but as with most great leaders there's a certain distance. He doesn't have to say much or do much, if somebody screwed up, for you to want the ground to open up and swallow you. He's a very intimidating personality, and that's why I sometimes love being his interpreter. I can joke when I leave this thing and say I had the most important two star general in the American army hanging on my every word.

I look at myself as fortunate because I am not in the direct line of fire; all I have to do is get a good night's sleep and show up to do the job. A bit easier than for some of those troops who are dealing with a lot more soldiers and intangibles, where a lot more can go wrong. I think the local generals get a kick out of it because they know, and everybody knows, that you have all kinds of ranks but you're not talking about equals in any objective sense. General Nash has got at his command forces here that could, in three

days, probably blow up and destroy all three Armies here. But he has never misused that, he has never been overbearing or disrespectful to them in any way – which could easily happen when you're in this kind of position when, 'Hey, you know, these are generals but you could kick their butt with one hand tied behind your back'.

He's always treated them with the utmost respect, completely as equals, trying very hard to get them to understand his position. He has never threatened them directly and I think they respect him because he treats them as equals. He loves to say, 'I'm just a soldier, I'm not a politician', and he really sticks to that. They respect his directness, his candour, the fact that his word is his bond and they can depend on it.

> **The ethnic thing is insane but we're living in the Middle Ages and that's why it's still alive.**

My personal view, if I take my uniform off for a minute, is that the people here will not be able to live in complete peace unless there is a big brother here sitting and making them play nice. That's what the Turks did, that's what the Austrians did and that's what Tito did. You can't undo that thousand years of history in one year, that's logic. Unless somebody comes here to play peace-maker with a big stick for a few years it's going to be tough. Contrary to popular belief it's not going to take that much. These people are not completely clueless, they know what the Americans can do. It's not going to take that large a NATO force remaining here to keep the peace. As long as they know that Aviano is not that far off, and we can bomb them before lunch, they're going to behave. But it does require resolve and staying and that's up to the politicians to decide.

I think it was a very noble thing that we did to come here. I came with very mixed feelings; I cursed this place, I tried to forget about this place but I ended up coming back here to try to help. On a human level I empathise with everybody on all three sides who suffered in this war. I see real criminals as individuals and some of these individuals are on all three sides. The ethnic thing is insane but we're living in the Middle Ages and that's why it's still alive.

At the bottom this war was about the same thing that every single war was about. An ancient Greek philosopher said, 'every single war is about money'. Stealing somebody else's land is basically the same thing, and that is what's at the root of this war. In the West it was not too long ago that we learned this lesson, fifty-seven years ago, but at least now it's commonly accepted that stealing your neighbour's land is not the way to enrich yourself. Wealth is now measured, in the West, not in land but in terms of something else; intellect, ingenuity, productivity. But here we are still back in that old mind-set. Tito played a master performance but, like every system based upon one personality, it was doomed. I personally think these countries should have been allowed to vote for their independence after the Second World War or, even better, after the First World War.

The real tragic thing is that the younger generation, people of my age, and I've met them from all the sides, will all tell you the same thing: when we were growing up, and I speak for myself as well as Serbs, Croats and Muslims, this ethnic thing was no big deal. We had friends from all three sides and there was just no ethnic hatred. But it didn't last long enough for the old generation, who had long memories, to die out. And I think that's partly a lot of what went on – there were too many people who wanted to re-fight World War Two."

Two Apache AH64 Attack helicopters return from dusk patrol along the Zone of Separation along the northern Posavina Corridor to Camp Hampton.

# Sergei Generalov

COLONEL, COMMANDER OF RUSSIAN BRIGADE

### Interviewed at US Camp Colt

"The unit that I command is fully manned, they have everything they need and the situation is stable. We are not experiencing any particular problems but maybe that's because we are airborne forces. I'm proud to be here, I'm proud to be a representative of Russia, I'm proud that General Nash, like it or not, has already entered the history of this state. If the conflicting sides don't right now understand the good things we are doing, I hope their children and grand-children will understand. This is a unique event – when our military is here for the sake of peace.

Our Brigade mans checkpoints, provides security and freedom of movement for citizens, observes and is present at mass burial sites and, by our presence here, provides freedom for democratic elections. Our mission is similar to the one being done by the Americans.When I first spoke to General Nash I said this is a unique case; history has shown us on the same side of the barricades only during the Second World War. For a lengthy period we were on opposite sides of the barricades. The experience of the work shows that we have found a common language. We understand each other not only as people but as professionals. The most important thing about our airborne troops is not necessarily strong muscles but a strong spirit. We also have two feet and two hands, we are the same kind of people as you are. We also want peace, we also want to communicate with each other, to talk to each other. You can be glad when people are not shooting at you."

# Brett Bartell

AAFES MANAGER,

### Interviewed at PX shop, Tuzla Airbase

"I wanted to be part of something instead of being somebody who says, 'Oh yeah, I'm part of AAFES and we were down there.' I wanted to be on the ground floor, one of the guys who actually did it. So I volunteered for the Macedonia mission but they didn't need anybody else and finally the mission for Bosnia came down and they picked me, promoted me to a manager and sent me on down here.

I was a Russian and Serbo-Croatian linguist in the Army for eight years. I was an interrogator with Military Intelligence. I'm from a very small town in Pennsylvania, my summer job was bailing hay. My father was a navy guy, in subs for ten years and he took that thing and turned it into a very lucrative career working for Nuclear Power. I started a college education at Penn State University but I ran out of money. So I joined the Army – originally for money for college – but I just lost interest in it and got a little more into what I was doing in the Army.

AAFES is a really great company. You're not going to find another company that is so orientated towards one mission and that is supporting the soldiers. I really don't think you could find any other retail business so keen on every aspect of this mission. The company is for that purpose. Of course we are a retail operation and trying to make money like

Top.
Colonel Generalov, the Commander of the Russian IFOR Brigade, inspects a US Army M1A1 Main Battle Tank while visiting Camp Colt with General Nash. The Russian Brigade falls under the command of the US Division.

Bottom.
A BTR Russian made Armoured Personnel Carrier at Ugljevik, the Russian Brigade HQ. Note the arm-patch which says 'Russia' in cyrillic script.

Overleaf.
Aerial view of Tuzla city.

everyone else but most of our money is used for these kinds of operations, covering extra transport costs and so on. It's mind boggling when you think of all the places that AAFES is; it's a world-wide company from everywhere from Guam to California. If you think of all the places where the United States military is there's always an AAFES there.

When we first came down here the troops were cheering as AAFES organic vehicles, with 'Earth Friendly' on the side, were crossing the Sava River. It was really a sight to see, something else. The first day we were open here the line was winding down the road for maybe a quarter of a mile. You would be surprised how much a six pack of soda and a bag of chips means to someone who's been eating MREs (Meals Ready to Eat) for three months. It's not the big things but the little things that make you feel at home.

I can't say enough about the local staff, I would take ten of them home with me if I could. They're fantastic, great workers, positive attitudes. You see something down here you don't see in the States. In the States a lot of people take their job for granted whereas these people here haven't had work and they really want to work. You'd be surprised at the difference between somebody who works because they have to work and somebody who works because they want to work. These people have no retail experience at all and they came in here totally willing to learn. They have really surprised me.

They are no different from anyone else. They just want to live and be happy, have kids and get married. They want what everyone else wants, and it doesn't matter where you go, they want no more than any other American, German, Italian. They want to be happy. I've come across prejudice like you come across it in the States. It's no stronger than blacks and whites in America, neo-Nazis and Jews in Germany. Everywhere you go you are going to have some prejudice, this is no different. It happens to be cultural and religious which is a different line of prejudice than you might see in the States. I feel prejudice is wrong but you are going to have it, people are people.

Everyone says there's a kind of euphoria at this shop here. It's hard to explain but every day you have something new going down and it makes you feel good. It's an airbase so there's a lot of people coming through. The Russians love it, it's just another sign that capitalism is on its way to Russia and they want what everyone else has got. They want the nice things in life.

We've had everything from senators to ambassadors here, three-star generals, everyone sooner or later comes to get something. I am of the belief that I treat all my customers with an equal amount of respect. That's because this is an environment where you get treated like a king whoever you are."

Top.
American soldiers queue up to be served at the PX shop at Tuzla airbase. Because the troops are not allowed to go off camp the PX shops are always busy.

Bottom.
Brett Bartell, a manager for AAFES in Bosnia, stands outside the PX shop at Tuzla airbase, HQ of US Army Task Force Eagle, with AAFES supervisor Maja Marjanovic.

# Maja Marjanovic

## AAFES SUPERVISOR

### Interviewed in PX shop, Tuzla Airbase

"I studied mechanical engineering in Sarajevo and when the war started I came home to Tuzla and they said I could finish my course here at the university. I almost did this but the Americans came and I got a job.

The education was good here before the war but now we don't have any kind of books, we learn from notes, sometimes the professor comes in and just reads from a book. It was very good throughout Yugoslavia. Eight years of primary school, everybody had to do it,

and then we had high schools: schools for nurses, electricians, mechanics, secretaries and teachers. My speciality was maths.

I was in Sarajevo when the war started. In March 1992 the Serbs blocked the town and closed it from all sides, all the people in the city were holding peace demonstrations. There were too many soldiers in Sarajevo: Serbs with red caps, Muslims with green caps and UN soldiers too. I never believed we would have war here. Since Tito died we had problems at Kosovo, in Slovenia and Croatia but never was it so important in my opinion, I always thought we can fix that.

I was kind of stupid because I believed in my world, I had my problems with school and that was most important for me. I didn't pay attention to anything else. I have friends of all nationalities and I never had any kind of problem with that. Suddenly we had war in the streets. I remember in a small town near Tuzla, Kalesija, thirty five kilometres away, the Serbs started to fight but I still didn't believe war was going to come here, to Tuzla. And then one day they started, somebody just pressed a button and it started. I'm not sure, to be honest, who started first, everybody was very nervous.

> I still didn't believe war was going to come here, to Tuzla. And then one day they started, somebody just pressed a button and it started. I'm not sure, to be honest, who started first, everybody was very nervous. When the first shell hit my neighbourhood I was at home about two o' clock in the morning. There was an alert and all the neighbours went down into the basement. It was a little bit normal because nobody was scared because we didn't know what you need to be scared of.

When the first shell hit my neighbourhood I was at home about two o' clock in the morning. There was an alert and all the neighbours went down into the basement. It was a little bit normal because nobody was scared because we didn't know what you need to be scared of. It was like you hear something far, far away from you and then you hear that sound, a whistle and then I have the feeling that everything was gone, that all the buildings are destroyed, that they destroyed everything that was on the ground. Terrible.

There were sand bags above us and as small pieces of shell started to hit them, the sand started to fall down and that was scary. Everybody was crying. For the first time in my life I saw my neighbour, she was about sixty five years old, crying. She was scared to death. There were some cars outside and they were hit too, fire everywhere. We spent the whole night in the shelter, everybody slept but me. I was scared to death, such an empty feeling because you don't have any explanation why they did it, you never know when they're going to repeat that. In a few minutes? Can you go home after a few hours or not?

And then the morning came and I went outside to check. There were such strange and powerful sounds of destruction, just like everything is crashed and destroyed, I mean really destroyed. I walked out and everything was normal, we just had a few holes in the street and everybody's windows were broken. I live on the fifth floor and we had glass all over the place, that was really scary. But after a few times you just get used to it. There were times when me and my friends just decided to go downtown and have a coffee and in those times you just don't think they can start to shell, and then they start and you run and try and find somewhere safe and then run home.

We survived a year without water and without electricity and we were happy to be alive. I did nothing, although I did attend some lessons at school. That was a really cold

experience because there was no heating. We would sit there in coats and gloves and then go home to be just a little bit warmer. We would sleep about sixteen hours a day. We had lots of satellite channels in town and we could see CNN reports or SKY reports and at the same time we could, until last summer, watch Serb television news. That was good because you heard from Bosnian television and then you heard the same stuff but a different story on the Serb television.

I think Tuzla is the safest area in the ex-Yugoslavia, in Bosnia for sure. That was just because we have political leaders like we have and Mayor Beslagic is leader of some kind of Social Democratic party and he has a lot of people who follow him. Because of that we didn't have any problems with the Croats around, or Serbs. I don't know anybody in town who had problems just because he was a Serb. About two thousand Serbs stayed behind in Tuzla and we have a lot of refugees now.

I'm surprised with how the Americans look. On TV they're tall, big people but here almost everyone is short, not tall. They're a little bit funny because they would like to be friendly with everybody. You have two types: those who are friendly with everybody and would like to know everything about you and your parents; and those who just stand behind you and they just ask for what they need. The Americans work hard. We in ex-Yugoslavia have eight hour working days but I notice they work for twelve maybe fourteen hours a day. They are great to work with."

# US ARMY 1ST BRIGADE

## In the Posavina Corridor

## Kenneth Black

ARMY CHEF AT 1ST BRIGADE HQ

**Interviewed at Camp Kime, near Brcko**

"I'm from Mississippi and I joined the Army in 1989. I guess I joined because I was looking for a little excitement, adventure and I had to make a little money at the same time – all three of those things. When I first joined it was strange, different. I had trouble adapting because they had strict rules and discipline. Before I joined, I was living a wild life, carefree; partying, hanging out with the fellas, friends, I was just wild. Army life kind of made me grow up a little bit, getting responsibility, taking more pride in what I do, build character, made me more responsible.

Mississippi is a very good place to be raised in. I had it kind of hard but that made me respect life more, respect the dollar more, to take pride in everything I do and to work hard for everything I got. Mississippi is a very agricultural state, we grow all different types of vegetables; peanuts, potato, okrey, string beans, green beans, canteloupes. I grew up in the type of family where everyone – grandmothers, uncles, aunts – all could cook really good so I had the opportunity to eat all kinds of scrumptious meals and that kind of led me to want to be a cook. I could do a number of different things before I arrived in the Army, such as making banana pudding, fried chicken, red beans and rice, Mississippi mud pie, numerous cakes, cookies, desserts, biscuits – you name it, if I've seen it done, I did it.

> Food is very important. Food is the morale of the soldiers – keep them warm, sheltered and give them food – I think these are the three most important morale boosters.

I'm responsible for preparing three hot meals a day for the headquarters of the First Brigade here at Kime Base. This involves everything from slicing meat to making salads, starches, vegetables, gravies, cool-aid, coffee. We get up in the morning two or three hours prior to the meal and use that as our preparation time to prepare a quality, well balanced meal for the soldiers. We have some local workers and they assist us to keep the place clean and sanitised, it's kind of fun working with them because we can learn a little of their language. They work good. We first arrived here in the winter time. It wasn't an unusual place but it was unusual because we had never been here before. It had trees, rocks, mountains, all that stuff like any normal place but us being here for the first time and the place being called Bosnia – that's really what made the difference.

Food is very important. Food is the morale of the soldiers – keep them warm, sheltered and give them food – I think these are the three most important morale boosters. Everyone says the food is excellent here, but the food is excellent because you have a bunch of professionals who take pride and time in the meals and the quality of the food that they prepare.

Everybody should take pride in their jobs: work hard at it, learn it, experience the ups and downs and the result will be a masterpiece. Food is one of my hobbies, I like

Kenneth Black, head chef at 1st Brigade HQ, located at Camp Kime near Brcko.

preparing it as much as I like eating it. I'm very pro-active, I like to work out. Everything I do I try to give it a hundred and ten per cent. It's like I'm on drugs but I'm not, it's all natural, I'm on fruits, barley juices, the good stuff."

# Gregory Fontenot

## COLONEL, COMMANDER OF 1ST BRIGADE

### Interviewed at Camp Kime

"I'm a soldier's son and unlike many others I had no desire to be a fireman or a doctor. I wanted to be a soldier from the first that I ever thought of my future. It's sort of a strange story but in the days that my father was a soldier we wore cotton fatigues with a herringbone pattern in them. The buttons were made of metal and each button had thirteen stars in it arranged in a five-pointed star. I asked him what the star was about, he talked about the constitution of the United States and the original thirteen colonies and I thought this is something important, this is something that I want to do.

I've never lost that child-like fascination with the idea of the United States Constitution and an army that stands for an eighteenth century idea that all of us are created equal. It's powerful to me, the notion that all of us are created equally and endowed by our Creator with certain inalienable rights, and this Army stands for that. It's a powerful idea, the notion of the eighteenth century Enlightenment. It's John Locke, the Tabula Rasa, the idea that we are born with a clean slate and what we make with our lives is what fills that slate. It's an original, American idea. Locke is the originator of the idea, but the execution of the notion that we are that way is profoundly American. It's what makes us who we are.

I don't hold with the notion that the United States has some special mission, although I think I did at one point. It turns out we have interests like everyone else, like Palmerston said: 'We have permanent interests and no permanent friends'. Because it's deeply rooted in our consciousness, the notion that there is right and wrong out there, despite your permanent interests, you try to do what's right and I think, to some extent, we've been successful.

I was born in Japan and grew up in the Army – in France and Germany and the United States, on different tours. My father went to Korea and I elected to stay in Kansas where I went to school at the Kansas State University and was commissioned through the Reserve Officers' Training Corps Programme in 1971 as an armour officer.

I commanded a tank battalion in Desert Storm and have since that time been the director of the School of Advanced Military Study at Fort Leavenworth and worked as Chief of Planning for the US Army's Training and Doctrine Command, the organisation responsible for thinking about what it is we are going to do in places like Bosnia and elsewhere, how the Army is going to organise itself and fight, what sort of weapons should it have, that kind of business. I took command of this outfit on the 7th of June 1995.

In Desert Storm I was surprised at how painful it was to lose soldiers. It's a deeply personal matter when you lose soldiers assigned to you. The other thing I was amazed by was the horrendous lethality of the modern battlefield. One second you're alive, the next you're dead, there's no in between. Weapons are so lethal now, in a high intensity conflict. The destruction is unbearable almost, it's just unbelievable.

Top.
US Army troops return
from patrol at Camp McGovern

Bottom.
Colonel Fontenot at Camp Colt.
In the background is an
Apache Attack helicopter.

On 26 February we attacked at 10.30 at night and we fought through two tank battalions and a couple of infantry companies that were dug in – until about 6.30 in the morning. The horrendous, instantaneous destruction of human life was amazing to me. The third most striking thing about Desert Storm was the horrendous disaster ecologically that the war created. I lived for six weeks in a place where, when the wind shifted, you had to have lights on to see what you were doing.

I wasn't so naive that I thought war was clean and easy, obviously it's not or people would feel differently about it than they do. The most striking memory I have is just what an outrageous, obscene waste of human life and treasure that Desert Storm was. But, if there was a just war in the late twentieth century, that was it, it was the right thing to do, it was just obscene. I felt great sorrow, genuinely felt pain at the loss of life on both sides.

Soldiers are by nature introspective. Any Army tends to be introspective because what you do matters in a permanent sort of way. If a company fails, people lose their jobs, there's tremendous social dislocation; if a unit in an army fails – it's terminal. It's pretty important stuff. When the United States Army came out of Vietnam, there was a temptation to assess the loss as not being our fault and I believe that argument could be made and would withstand the test of time. But the Army said there were things here that were our fault and what we need to do is take a good hard look at how we do business. There are generations of officers who have been moulded by the idea of 'let's not become captured by systems which don't work – let's examine our systems'.

> The most striking memory I have is just what an outrageous, obscene waste of human life and treasure that Desert Storm was. But, if there was a just war in the late twentieth century, that was it, it was the right thing to do, it was just obscene.

There were some tremendous lessons from Desert Storm. It was an industrial age war in the sense that production of weapons and numbers of weapons still mattered. It was an information age war in that the ability to move information around the battlefield rapidly, and the scientific miracle of satellite navigation, enabled us to operate in the desert in ways that were incomprehensible to the Iraqis. That's why this war was over so quickly; it's not that they didn't fight, they did fight but they were out-matched by our weaponry and they were out-matched by us intellectually and they were outmatched by a fairly bold decision to go way out into the desert.

The future of warfare, given that weapons' lethality is going to increase not decrease, is concerned with the question, 'How do you minimise the number of people on a battlefield?' There's a guy who's written a book called *The Empty Battlefield*; battlefields are getting emptier but they're not empty yet. I think that's the direction the future will go – the ability to move the information around the battlefield will be more important than the number of weapons you bring to the battlefield.

It's the age-old problem of how do you mass effects – that's how you win. In the eighteenth century you did it by massing the soldiers, literally they stood shoulder to shoulder and fired muzzle loading, smooth bore 50 calibre musket balls which weren't accurate at all. You had to be close and have a bunch of you together to achieve any real target effect. That's not how it is any more and to fail to understand that is to cause lots of your own people to be killed.

My first impression of Bosnia was that it wasn't quite as horrible as I'd expected, in terms of the level of destruction. The other impression I have is that it's not Europe, it's

Top.
A member of the American 'Medivac' helicopter crew looks down on a destroyed bridge over the River Sava.

Bottom.
Members of 1st Brigade at ease after blowing a bunker in the Zone of Separation.

not European at all, it's tribal, it's mediaeval, it's feudal with neo-Stalinist governments. There's this hill country fable in the United States about the Hatfields and the McCoys that wage this internecine warfare between their families in the hills. That's Bosnia but with tanks and RPG-7s.

I think it happened because of crass miscalculation on the part of the governments. Tudjman, Milosevic, Izetbegovic – all of them in my opinion bear great responsibility for what's happened here. Arguably, if it's OK to secede from Yugoslavia then why shouldn't the Serbs be able to secede from Bosnia? Same argument that Alija Izetbegovic made, Karadzic tried to make. There was no effort from the beginning for any genuine negotiation among the parties and it got out of hand. Europe stood by, everyone, including the United States, stood by.

Dayton is a process of negotiation and discussion, it is not an end-state. It has a formula which I think is fairly sound, it says freedom of movement will promote reconstruction and these two things together will promote reconciliation. It places the burden for peace where it ought to be – on the parties and not on the international community. The international community didn't cause the war and it isn't going to be able to stop the war, it's up to the parties to do that. Freedom of movement is not a reality everywhere in the country, but I had one hundred and five thousand people traverse the Posavina corridor last month. Each month it increases. The open market at checkpoint Alpha 2 is demonstrably a statement by normal people that they wish to get on with their lives. It gets about fifteen hundred people on weekends and about five hundred on weekdays. Everywhere we are you can see them selling things to each other.

Does that mean anyone here has become a Jeffersonian democrat, the enlightened age democrat? Of course not. Are they going to change? Are their ethnic hatreds going to recede, are they going to trust each other? They haven't for several hundred years, I see no reason why they will change in a year. But there's hope. In my opinion, Brcko is a linchpin to making this work and the reason is that the Republika Srpska entity within Bosnia, to be able to work, needs to be able to communicate between Pale and Banja Luka and the Serbs don't expect to be able to cross Federation territory. So they need access to the Posavina corridor and Brcko is the linchpin of that access. On the other hand, the Federation looks at Brcko as a natural economic and trading entrepot for Northern Bosnia, a fair assessment. So they need to be able to traverse Brcko and hopefully get the railway bridge built up which gets you to the railway yards in Croatia, which then gets you to Belgrade, Zagreb and the rest of Europe. The barge port on the Sava in Brcko gets you access to the Danube and the rest of Europe, so it's very important to the Federation.

If there's some possibility of economic co-operation, if not reconciliation, in Brcko, then that's the key to making it work. The key is to come to some reasonable accommodation of the competing interests of the two sides vis-à-vis Brcko. I don't believe, however, that you can glibly hand over Brcko to either the Serbs or the Federation. That's something they're going to have to decide for themselves and I'm glad I don't have to make the decision.

I'm too close to the problem to be a reliable or useful estimator of the future. I'm manic depressive about Bosnia – one day I think it's going to work and the next I don't. All I know is to focus on creating the conditions to allow engagement, to me you have to keep them talking. I'm not going to educate them out of this mediaeval idea of fiefdoms in a year, but there will be people behind me in non-governmental organisations and the UN, whoever's mandated to continue the Dayton process. This worked because we came in prepared to fight, looks count in this environment. In the early days there was a lot of

speculative and half condescending laughter about American troops coming in, heavily armoured and weapons at the ready at all times. That's the way we train and live elsewhere. After about two months you begin to hear tones of grudging respect for that decision and within about four months there was 'hey, this is the right thing to do because it is consistent with the way you guys operate'. It is compelling in that 'these guys are always ready, they're serious about this'. The Army had the courage not to get upset or sensitive or defensive about our style of approach.

We changed our doctrine after Desert Storm and said, 'What we really need to be is versatile'. We had to make that an objective for the institution. I think versatility is absolutely essential here, you have to be able to move from a combat environment to a peace compliance environment, and you have to expect your folks to be at home either with the media, at least willing to spend time with the media, or working in Joint Military Commissions, in which the skills of a negotiator are what's essential.

Integrity in these operations is decisive. These guys continue to be amazed at the fact that we tell them the truth. They're always looking for a hidden agenda, because that's how they routinely operate: dissembling, lying, misrepresenting. I think this is how they've operated all their lives, certainly in the last four years. They're confounded by the notion of people telling them the truth.

I can't think about after this, I can't imagine not being in Bosnia. Bosnia is my life. But I'm not a Balkan junkie, there's a lot of Balkan junkies here and, quite frankly, I don't understand them. Maybe it's a sort of rubber-necking fascination; there's been a car accident and you slow down and say, 'Golly, isn't that gross'. I can't account for it in any other way.

There are a number of people who have this genuine commitment to do something for people in trouble. I respect and admire these people. I don't have that kind of commitment where, whenever there's a disaster, I rush to that scene. Thank God there are people who feel that way. I see them and work with them every day. Norwegian Relief, Swedish Rescue Services, all these NGOs you run into.

The UN High Commissioner for Refugees is the key player, the implementor of the civil side of the treaty in my area at least. We have very talented people working with us. Salvattore Lombardo in Tuzla – an expert at working his way through this stuff, he understands the area fairly well, he has a good grasp on how to run a meeting in which the issues are contentious and difficult. Salvattore and UNHCR, as Ombudsman for these organisations, has helped bring some synchronisation and harmony and an ability to focus on getting out and doing the work. So there isn't redundant work being done, there isn't duplication of effort – and that is powerful.

I don't want to take on the role of some sort of warlord of the Posavina who tells people what must be done, but rather I want to facilitate and work myself out of a job, give the civilian folks an opportunity to synchronise the efforts themselves. We're not going to impose a military chain of command on civilians, it's just not going to work, they would have joined the military if they liked that kind of thing. What we can do, however, is suggest and let them develop their strategy and their campaign for making it happen in

> These guys continue to be amazed at the fact that we tell them the truth. They're always looking for a hidden agenda, because that's how they routinely operate: dissembling, lying, misrepresenting. I think this is how they've operated all their lives, certainly in the last four years. They're confounded by the notion of people telling them the truth.

which they accept responsibility.

You can't keep armed troops here for two to three decades, you could but it would solve nothing if you don't deal with the root of the issue here, which is: how do you get people back to work? How do you get the infrastructure moving in such a way that it can sustain people working? And how do you promote the difficult concept of understanding that just because somebody's different from you he doesn't have to be killed? We're talking about policies and principles of democracy, principles of human rights that aren't understood here and you can't do that with guys with bayonets. Guys with bayonets don't teach that, they can make the conditions possible so it can be taught but you need someone who isn't armed to the teeth to teach them. When I'm walking around with a pistol talking about the Constitution of the United States, it's a picture that's a little incongruous. Civilians need to do that and we need to create the conditions for them to do it.

I think the future in Bosnia has possibilities. I'm too close to it to suggest which of the several possibilities will be realised. You ask me tomorrow and I might be all bubbly and enthusiastic and say, 'Oh yeah, peace is going to work', but the truth is what we have now is not peace, what we have now is armistice. The business of the military here is to create the conditions to allow the process to work, the business of the civilians is to get the process, the heart of the process, under way and to sustain it over time so it can succeed. If we can do those things I will go home from this mission with a feeling of success."

# Susan Gregory

PRIVATE, SECRETARY TO COLONEL FONTENOT

### Interviewed at Camp Kime

"I'm from a little town upstate New York. I always said I was going to join the military. It was easy for me because I wanted to prove myself. A lot of people said, 'you'll never make it' but I joined and I did make it.

Sometimes I ask myself what am I doing here. So far it's not bad at all. I've met females who say they get treated worse than men, they say guys don't want to look up to a female, but from what I've seen so far they treat us the same. I do all the Colonel's paperwork, do his schedule, answer his phone. It's great, he's the nicest man I've ever met. Him and Sergeant Baker, they treat me really good. The night me and Colonel Fontenot danced in front of the whole headquarters was probably the most interesting moment. It was fun, I wasn't expecting it, he just grabbed me and pulled me up there in front of everyone, we were the only ones dancing.

I've learned more in the last seven months than I have in my whole life: the way the world is, a lot of things. You meet a lot of people, I'm glad we're here, I've seen a lot of changes. When we first got here not a lot of people were out, now everybody's out and kids wave and chase our vehicles. They're starting to go to school again. I hope they can stay at peace.

I am probably going to stay in the Army for twenty years. I want to be a Sergeant Major, I want to see how far I can get. If a female tries she can do it."

Top.
Susan Gregory, Secretary to Brigade Commander Colonel Fontenot.

Bottom.
1st Brigade Infantry and Engineers patrol in single file through a suspected minefield, on their way to blow up a bunker.

# Jelena Bukarica

### TRANSLATOR FOR US ARMY 1ST BRIGADE

#### Interviewed at Camp Kime

"I was born in Croatia on the 28th of May 1966. I lived all my life in Croatia and then the war broke out. My father comes from a mixed Serbian-Croat family so he was declaring himself as a Yugoslav, but when the war broke out, and everybody was supposed to be somebody, he was declared a Croatian. My mother is a pure Macedonian. So I was also a Yugoslav, which means I would feel I had offended my father if I said I was a Macedonian and offend my mother if I said I was a Croatian. I don't have the feeling that I belong to either of these nationalities.

I was baptised in an Orthodox church in Macedonia when I was two years old so I really don't know who I belong to. When they ask me what I am I try and avoid the question and say, 'Don't worry about that'. If I cannot avoid that I have to lie, just in order to avoid conflict.

I was living in the Krajina region and I started working in the Kenyan Battalion as an interpreter. I was staying there until August '95 when all the Serbs fled as refugees. Over 150,000 of them. Most went to Serbia and my parents went there too. My father was a former officer in the JNA and he believed in that so he decided to stay on the Serbian side. Whoever got the idea of dividing my country – Yugoslavia – I blame them for everything. I used to have my country, now I don't have a country. I don't belong to Croatia because they won't let me go back because we were living in the Serb part of Krajina. In Serbia it's even worse; we are refugees, forgotten by everybody, nobody thinks about us except the people who deliver the humanitarian aid we get once a month.

I don't know much about Bosnia, I don't see anything good that might happen to me here, I don't belong anywhere although I would like to go back to my home in Croatia. In Serbia, there are so many refugees, they are sick of us. If they don't hate us, they certainly don't like us. It's very very difficult to get a job there. I have a degree in economics. I finished my degree in Mostar in 1989 – but at that time everything was preparing for war so I never had a chance to work in my profession. When I visited my parents in Belgrade, my aunt, who lives in Brcko, called me here and said the Americans were looking for translators. I'm coming from the Serbian side to a Croatian-held area.

When I signed a contract it said we have to work seven days a week with no days off, unless the officers give you a day off. It also said we have to live in a camp and wear a uniform, helmets and flackjackets. The job itself is a new experience because I live in a camp and I find it really interesting and an adventure to work with the Americans. With the UN even the kids were making fun of them.

My usual working day starts at 6 o'clock in the morning. The job is interesting, I don't complain, I only complain about the weather when it's too hot or too cold. They are polite, they are gentlemen – although I heard that gentlemen never wear green – and they are co-operative. I really like working with them. I would like to go somewhere abroad, to any English-speaking country, because I don't belong to this country. I would like to go to the States.

I can see this problem is going to be repeated again and again and will come back in a few years. I don't think it can be solved once and for ever. The Roman Empire, the Turkish, Austrian Empires, everybody had their interest here, in this country and everybody will try and get use of this country. I hate that idea.

Top left.
Jelena Bukarica, a translator from Croatia now working for the US Army at Camp Kime.

Top right.
US Army engineers use their skills to establish their exact location, on the road known as 'Route Desolation'.

Bottom.
1st Brigade engineers pick their way through the hundreds of miles of trenches that criss-cross the country.

My father was born in 1944 and three months later his father was killed in the war. His father was killed as a Partisan, one of Tito's soldiers. If he had a son – we are two sisters – and he had to fight, he would have been killed also in this war. Does that mean my child is going to be killed in fifty years' time or twenty? My grand-mother experienced two world wars and two Balkan wars. That's too much for a human being. I cannot see why this will not happen again and that is why I would like to leave this area. I have to do something about it."

# Michael Emory

## CORPORAL
## TEAM LEADER/COMPANY SNIPER, 5TH CAVALRY REGIMENT

### Interviewed at Brcko Bridge

"Our job here in Brcko is to enforce the Dayton Peace Accord and control the bridge between Croatia and Brcko. Initially we were very apprehensive, aware of mines and the threat from bombs and snipers. It started out exciting, a car drives by too fast; you were ready to do something. Now we've become complacent, now we know more the people in the area, we're more familiar with the customs. You pick up some words, you learn people's names and they're more friendly towards you.

We're not supposed to have friends though, we're not like the British, French or Swedish soldiers – we're not supposed to drink, we're not supposed to fraternise with any of the locals whatsoever. But it's nature, curiosity, to do that. You meet more and more people and more and more people want to meet you, they come here out of curiosity. When I first went on patrol around Brcko I had known so many people just from standing here that I was excited to get out and actually be in the area with those people. We don't get to walk around. If we want to go see some place we're not allowed to do that, and that is extremely wearing on the brain. It's terrible.

It's not that I don't like Private Wyman here, but all you do is speak to Wyman all day long, and you're in some foreign country. It would be as if some alien civilisation landed in Texas and all you could do is look at the spaceship and all of a sudden it took off. That's what it's like, to be an American soldier in Bosnia sucks. It's a prison camp.

What I've been told time and time again is that when people first see us they cannot get past our equipment, our flackvests, our protective masks. They see us walking with our weapons, we're not supposed to look threatening or provocative in any way, but they say we do. Every time we do a patrol debrief that's what we include in there, because that's what they tell us. As a patrol leader I asked the police what do the people feel, what's the general attitude towards IFOR doing patrols here, and they say, 'Well, if you people weren't pointing guns in all directions, and looking like you were ready to attack at any moment, everything would be fine.'

In Macedonia we patrolled the border between Serbia and Macedonia. I have never, and nobody here has either, ever seen anybody point a weapon at us in Brcko. In Macedonia it was almost a weekly occurrence that there was a Serbian sniper in the mountain pointing a weapon at us. We could see him but we didn't wear helmets, we didn't wear flackvests, we could go downtown and drink, we could wear civilian clothes. What's the difference between Macedonia and here? Nobody has ever been the least bit threatening towards us – they offer us beer.

1st Brigade engineer plants explosives in a command bunker on a former confrontation line near Brcko.

I have a dress that the man across the street gave me for my wife; I have countless pieces of equipment: uniforms, patches, knives that they just give to me because they say 'you Americans are nothing like what we thought. We thought you were coming down here and were going to be all mean and everything but here you are shaking hands and hugging and stuff like that – with Serbians'.

One day we were walking through the city and were standing in front of the police station, waiting for the Serbian police escort. We were talking with all these guys: Niko, Celo, Jovica, all these Serb guys that really like us, and we like them. We were sweating, sweat pouring off our faces, all over the place. And here goes a bunch of British guys, walking down the street with beers in their hands. No helmet, no weapon, no flakvest, no protective mask, nothing. Here we are looking at them and they say, 'Hey, how's it going?'. Yeah, it's going real nice – for you.

The local people say to us how come the British soldiers get to do this and we don't. How come we see the British soldiers drunk in the discos and you're not. Then you say to them because our commanders are idiots, they don't trust us, they think we're children. I'm twenty four years old, and yeah, I like to drink, I like to get a little crazy once in a while. It's like with a little kid: 'Don't touch the cookies on the shelf.' The kid's going to touch the cookies and he's probably going to break the jar, but if you let the kid have a couple of cookies once in a while he'll get used to it and pretty soon forget about the cookies. I don't think it's discipline so much as fear, nobody's going to risk their career or possibly go to jail. If you get caught drinking, that's disobeying a general order, from the General. Disobey a general order, maximum penalty for that – jail. Nobody's going to risk that.

> 'you Americans are nothing like what we thought. We thought you were coming down here and were going to be all mean and everything but here you are shaking hands and hugging and stuff like that – with Serbians'.

Macedonia is a great place, a beautiful country, nice people – it's got high mountains. I would rather spend a year and a half in Macedonia than what I've spent here. We were treated more professionally there, trusted more. If it was run by Americans it would be like this, but it was run by the UN, a Norwegian general. He was a good guy.

It was written in the newspaper in Brcko that the Chief of Police, when he heard the Americans were coming, said, 'We could fight them out there, maybe lose, maybe win and be a great nation, a top nation, but if we fight the Americans and lose, at least they will rebuild our country.' That's what it said in the newspaper, quite an interesting article.

I talked to the Chief of Police the day before yesterday, he's like the top dog here. I don't know the Mayor's name, but I do know the Chief of Police's name. He said, 'We didn't want a war, us people didn't want a war, our leaders decided we would have a war'. He's a really nice guy, I had coffee with him and he didn't have to do that, he didn't even have to see me."

# Todd Semonite

### LT COLONEL, CHIEF ENGINEER OF 1ST BRIGADE

**Interviewed near Brcko**

"I'm doing what I like which is engineering. I'm the kind of guy who likes to put things up, I like to see completion, I like to see how things come together. My boots are dirty

most of the time. We came across the Sava River the very first day and what my guys had to do was to break through the ZOS (Zone of Separation). The ZOS was impenetrable at that stage; we compare it to the German Lines in the First World War. Our engineers had to break holes through this band and we took four days, right in the very early part of January, breaking the roads through. Everywhere where the road went through the ZOS there was a whole mess of minefields in the middle of it; there were trenches that broke the road up, or great big piles of dirt.

So we took engineering teams, one on each side, with the opposing factions, put the factions into orange suits so they wouldn't shoot each other and we would say 'GO'. At nine o'clock in the morning one team would come from the south and one would come from the north and we would go in and clear mines, plough down the dirt and we would work right through to the very middle line, and when we got there you would see the factions almost shake hands. We opened up sixteen roads in four days in January, the patrols could go back and forth and it enhanced IFOR's freedom of movement. We continued on through the mission and we have opened up a total of forty two roads throughout the sector.

> We've blown up two thousand bunkers, that's a lot of bunkers. It's good work for my guys and enhances our training. We're going to make it so it's hard for these guys to go back to war.

My battalion is working inside the Zone of Separation where we work at clearing minefields. We have removed six hundred to date out of two thousand in the sector. There is a trenchline going all the way through this ZOS and we are trying to decimate it by blowing up bunkers. This is a World War One trenchline with bunkers built into it. We've blown up two thousand bunkers, that's a lot of bunkers. It's good work for my guys and enhances our training. We're going to make it so it's hard for these guys to go back to war.

One of the things that we have to track very carefully is that the destruction of that trenchline is uniform on both sides. If one side is not doing his work and the other side is, then the side doing the work has, in essence, opened up a flank, he has now made himself vulnerable. Now the whole ZOS is, in essence, open and there is more freedom of movement every day. In January when we came there were no civilian vehicles on the road at all, nowhere. It was quiet. You would see some inside the corridor where it's all Serb but as far as anything going north or south – it didn't exist.

I think that peace comes when people are happy and people are normally happy when they're secure and when they have money. We found, in some places, just the economic viability of an area really helps stabilise it. Down at Gradacac there's a lot of things going on, there's a lot of talk back and forth between the two sides; they're getting some economic joint ventures going; sharing of power, sharing of telephone lines. Anytime we can get something which crosses this line – a telephone, power, rail line or road – not only are there advantages of economic improvement but you also have the two sides coming together.

Very easily you could have both of the sides live on different sides of the line and never talk to each other, completely separate. But the Dayton Accord says this is going to be one country, therefore one of our jobs is to facilitate those things which can bring these two sides together."

# Tara Liana Smetak

ARMY COOK AT 1ST BRIGADE HQ

**Interviewed at Camp Kime**

"I joined the Army as a spur of the moment decision. I was working as a nurse's assistant and I didn't want to worry about paying back college loans. The Army isn't like anything I've ever experienced before. I'd met the same kind of people when I was growing up in Wisconsin, but when I joined the army there were people from all over the country. The great thing about the Army is that it's kind of like a small town.

There was nothing when we first came here. There was no camp set up, we were cooking off a trailer – plus we're soldiers so we had to pull guard duty, set up the tents we had to sleep in and get the meals out to the soldiers. The days were extremely long, extremely hard, everybody was tired, dirty. Now everything's got better; the living conditions, the morale. Now we've got showers, good food.

The food gets kind of repetitive here. We get chicken, a lot of beef products, the main starches are mashed potatoes, rice, noodles, all different kinds of noodles. I didn't want to be here at first but working with the civilians has made me think it's a good thing we're doing here. They're great, they're funny, they seem to really respect us. They tell us stories about how it was before we came, kind of sad and you can't help but start caring for them. They work so hard, they're so motivated, you just ask them to do something and it's done.

Wisconsin is the 'Cheese State' – lots of cows, farming lands, fishing, hunting, recreation. I think it was the best place to be raised because I wasn't exposed to a lot of cruelties in life, this maybe made me naive but the Army definitely fixed that. The Army experience has made me appreciate home. When I went home on R&R leave everything meant so much more than before. After the Army I'm going to school to do psychology, that's what I've always wanted to do. I'm twenty and I'm going to stay in until Valentine's Day 1999."

Top.
Colonel Semonite, chief
engineer of 1st Brigade,
by his armoured Humvee, after
a short visit to the 'free market'
in the shadow of IFOR checkpoint
Alpha 2 on Route Arizona.

Bottom.
Tara Smetak, US Army Chef,
in the catering office at Camp Kime.

## US ARMY 2ND BRIGADE

## The Badlands: Eastern Bosnia, including the Srebrenica area.

# William Huglund

FORENSIC CONSULTANT
SITE MANAGER AT SRPSKA VALLEY MASS GRAVE

### Interviewed at first mass grave dig, near Srebrenica

"We are collecting for evidence from mass graves. In the Srebrenica area we will look at four to six graves and then move on to eastern Croatia to look at a grave at Vukovar. As regards the graves themselves, we are assessing the number of individuals involved, the kinds of individuals that might be involved and, from the bodies themselves, we wish to obtain their age, the sex, the patterns of injuries they may have received, how they came about their deaths – and then hopefully some families can be reunited with some individuals that are missing. IFOR is guaranteeing personal security to the team.

We've been here for eight or nine days now. The first thing we had to do was de-mine the grave and document it photographically, videotape it, map the site and then begin to define the grave itself. We're looking at the inhabitants of the grave; the grave has a story to tell of the individuals and the grave itself has a story to tell. Our job is to get complete individuals out of the grave, the more complete the body the more complete the story it has to tell. You can't tell patterns of injuries if you only have part of them.

We have removed eighty individuals from the grave and we will probably have removed in excess of one hundred when we're done in the next couple of days. The individuals are attired in civilian clothing, many of them have wires around their wrists, their hands behind their backs. The context of this scene is consistent with the scenario that would indicate that the individuals who were victims were placed along the side of the road with the down sloping embankment, and the other individuals on the other side of the grave had probably shot them.

I don't know when this whole process will be finished. When you're talking about the graves we're up against a weather barrier in September sometime . . . the process in The Hague will, I imagine, be going on in the upcoming years. The personal security offered by IFOR has been very good and we get to stay on an Army Base – Camp Lisa – and the food is wonderful and the sleeping accommodation is very good too. It's interesting to see how they work and to talk to the fellas. They're very well organised and I'm always amazed at the military's ability to get things together and be rational about things. It's nice to meet these guys from all over the United States. It's starting to get a little lonely now and I like to talk about home.

I'm from Seattle, Washington and for the last sixteen years I've been Chief Medical

> We have removed eighty individuals from the grave and we will probably have removed in excess of one hundred when we're done in the next couple of days. The individuals are attired in civilian clothing, many of them have wires around their wrists, their hands behind their backs.

Top.
A convoy of US Army trucks kicks up a dust cloud on the road to Camp Demi. Note the typical Bosnian haystacks on the left.

Bottom right.
American 2nd Brigade Bradley's on patrol on a high bit of land above Kladanj.

Examiner with the King County Medical Examiner's Office in Seattle. For the past three or four years I've been doing missions on my vacations for Physicians for Human Rights, that's how I got into this. I made the choice and quit my job and took a contract for doing this for a year. It's challenging when you look at it from the standpoint of just the profession, the sheer magnitude and amount of remains that you're looking at, but I also think it's the right thing to do.

It's a puzzle to figure out, it's something that has some immediate satisfaction in that you're able to identify an individual and return them to their families. You collect evidence that might go into a trial that would, hopefully, make the people that are responsible, accountable. In the long run if people become accountable for their actions, maybe in the future they won't take advantage of the people they should be protecting, people in their own populations."

## Robert Boswell

### STAFF SERGEANT, US ARMY SCOUTS, 4-12 INFANTRY

**Interviewed at mass grave excavation site**

"My dad was a Sergeant Major and I figured if I was going to be treated like a soldier I might as well get paid for it. In 1967 I went through training, and then right into Vietnam for two and a half years. I went through five major campaigns, two Tet Offensives, I worked with the 101st a lot and then went to the 173rd Airborne Brigade as a Door Gunner. I spent a year there and then I came home and got out. I was a little bit fed up with war. It was like being scared twenty four hours a day, working with a bunch of people you knew were going to get killed sooner or later, surviving day to day.

The soldiers we have today are more intelligent, they ask too many questions, they don't follow instructions quite like the old soldiers did. We don't have that cross section of soldiers we used to have, everyone was drafted then, now they're all volunteers and I guess they have a reason to ask why. I don't know. It's not blind faith anymore, you can't just expect a soldier to trust you, you have to earn their respect and their trust.

I then worked in construction all over the States, concrete work, for sixteen years. I had some unresolved things in my life and I figured I'd go back to the place where my problems started and work them out, so I re-enlisted. I was kind of anti-social and violent and I figured I could work out some of the problems that I had, and I did.

We didn't know what to expect when we crossed the Sava River. We were uploaded and ready for anything we were going to run into. The people on the Muslim side of the thing were pretty friendly, the people on the Serb side weren't; but we didn't know either side at the time. As Scouts we were out all the time, we hit just about every road in this brigade. We saw a lot of armed people when we first got here, a lot of destruction.

A lot of it wasn't what I thought it was going to be, starting with starving people. I haven't seen a starving person since I've been here. I've seen a lot of people who are basically traumatised by this thing, guys who have seen a lot, have that thousand metre stare in their faces, they're sceptical of everyone they meet – it's like people that have got burned one way or another by the system.

I think the world community has let this whole country down. We should have been here a lot earlier, we could have stopped a lot of the atrocities that went on. I don't think

A forensic specialist from Physicians for Human Rights sits at the top of a mass grave, the first to be exhumed, near Srebrenica. The evidence these specialists gather will be given to the War Crimes Tribunal in The Hague, Holland, for possible use in a trial against indicted war criminals. Over a hundred bodies were found in this one grave.

the world community has the balls for stepping in on a mass scale to end conflicts like this. I think after Peace Accords are signed and agreements are made then forces go in, at one time or another the world community itself has to say 'to hell with it, enough of this, we've got to just stop it'. There's enough force in the world, and you know there is, to stop a conflict or at least to separate the forces.

Since Vietnam, the American public hasn't had enough balls to lose people. I think the country was basically neutered by the Vietnam War; it was the first war that was in their face, publicised on TV every night, casualty counts, body bags. I don't think the country has the guts for another one of those things. So, they're sceptical every time they send our soldiers to another country, and so far everything's worked out, not a soldier's been killed, but I think the whole thing would change if they saw a whole lot of soldiers die.

> **I don't think IFOR can pull out, I don't think the world would accept another Civil War in Yugoslavia – and that's the only reason they're not pulling out.**

We found out in Somalia you don't go after somebody unless you're prepared to. Not to say we don't have enough firepower to go find somebody but that's not the mandate. I think there's enough blaming to go round, enough finger pointing in this war for everybody. I think every one of these people has a bit of the blame to carry.

As Scouts we get out among these people a lot more than anyone else in the whole goddamn Task Force. We're in the middle of these people all the time, we've made friends on the Serb and Muslim sides. These people here are going to have to want peace and if they don't want peace, it ain't never going to be here. I think the people in general want peace, but I don't think it's profitable for the leaders to have peace, they lose their chunk of the pie. I think a new generation has to come up and change the way these people think. What I see is that these people act like a bunch of sheep, they have one big ram with a bell round his neck and he rings it and they follow.

I don't think IFOR's going to pull out of this place at all, not for a long time to come. I think there will be a reduced presence. I don't think IFOR can pull out, I don't think the world would accept another Civil War in Yugoslavia – and that's the only reason they're not pulling out. Everyone you ever talk to here says as soon as you're gone the shit's going to hit the fan. We hear it all the time and we talk to these people, we talk to both sides.

We're the eyes and ears of the Task Force. The Scouts are highly visible and highly motivated and they're different for the simple reason that they're put in the front of everything. We're the most mobile force the Task Force has. We're used to the max, we have the highest mileage rates, the highest everything rates, anytime there's anything to do the scouts are involved. We've been running over mines all winter long, they had just frozen, and now we're told we can't run on those roads. We've had people hanging off cliffs because the road's given way, we've frozen to the bottom of our vehicles this winter because we had no heaters. You tell me how you keep a group of people motivated enough to do their mission in circumstances like this.

They fear me more than they fear the enemy. No, I don't think they fear me, they trust me. They know that whatever I'm going to do I'm not going to get them hurt and if there happens to be shit going on they know they can count on me to get them out of it. If one of my men was hit, I would not leave them alone, I would get them out of there, no matter if I put myself at risk and I'm not a goddamn hero by any stretch of the imagination. When my guys were deployed here I promised them all that we would go back together, and that's what I meant.

Top.
Senior Airman Michael Folch of the USAF (United States Air Force) takes a walk amongst the Humvees of the 4-12 Regiment Scouts, at the mass grave site near Srebrenica. Sergeant Boswell can be see in the background. Senior Airman Folch can call up and control air assets if required by the ground commander.

Bottom.
4-12 Infantry and Engineers head off into the hills towards the former frontline between the Bosnians and the Serbs, near Kladanj. They always walk in single file because of the threat from landmines.

50

I see there are Muslims training, preparing for when IFOR leaves. They're training their asses off. When we first came here there were no disciplined soldiers on the Muslim side, we ran into two Mujahadeen type individuals but the majority of soldiers weren't well trained. But you go into the Muslim side now and they're training and they're training hard and they're well equipped, they're getting more equipment.

On the Serb side I don't see them training, all I see is stockpiling. They're hoarding arms and on the other side they're training. Both of these sides here are preparing for another war. I think both sides of this conflict don't think that peace is going to last and they're going to fight another war; but I think the only difference is that the Muslims are going to have the upper hand in the next one. Hopefully, the balance of power will shift enough so the bosses on the Serbian side will realise that if they go to war they will lose, and then they will make peace.

> I think both sides of this conflict don't think that peace is going to last and they're going to fight another war; but I think the only difference is that the Muslims are going to have the upper hand in the next one.

I don't keep my soldiers motivated, I keep them occupied and that keeps them motivated. They keep me motivated actually, they keep me laughing. I've got two of the biggest assholes on earth working for me right here, but we keep each other moving. He thinks I'm the anti-christ, my driver, he thinks he will burn in hell if he doesn't do what I tell him. I heard that Tito was a dictator and all that shit, but he kept them in line. When he died they lost all direction. I don't think most of these leaders give a shit about their people, and if they cared they would get out and look at what the hell's going on.

Hopefully Mladic will shoot himself. I don't think the people would bitch if we took Karadzic because they believe he stabbed them in the back at Dayton. But Mladic, I was told, attempted suicide once and maybe he'll carry it out this time, and do it right, and save IFOR a lot of problems. End it, and make the world a bright and shiny place."

# Anthony D. Washington

TECHNICAL SERGEANT,
ETAC (ENLISTED TERMINAL AIR CONTROLLER) USAF

**Interviewed at Camp Demi**

"Our responsibilities are to advise the Army ground commanders on the capabilities of Close Air Support. We also advise on mission planning and actually go out and control air assets, if needed. My sidekick here is Senior Airman Folch.

We have A-10s which is the aircraft we can use for close in work. They have a 30 millimetre gun and can engage targets close-in without threatening friendlies. We also have Navy aircraft, the F18s; we have the Mirage 2000 which is a French plane, the Tornados, the F15 Strike Eagles and we can't forget the Harriers – a British plane. We also have the AC-130 gunship which is the world's baddest aircraft, that thing can do more damage in one spot than anything in the world. It's a transport plane that they converted into a gunship: it's got a very powerful 105mm canon, a Howitzer; it's basically a flying tank.

Top
Sergeant Anthony D. Washington of the United States Air Force, communicating with fighter aircraft in his role as CAS (Close Air Support) liaison for the groung commander of thr 4-12 infantry.

Bottom.
The road to Camp Demi, on the road between Vlasnica and Kladanj.

We have a lot of firepower at our disposal here. You want them to come in quick because you always want to have that element of surprise, it can give you the upper hand. They're like, 'What the hell? What hit us? What's happening?' A lot of times we go out on patrol and we don't know what we're going to face, but you've always got to have that situational awareness for anything that may come up. They seem to comply when they see those aircraft overhead because they keep thinking about when they got bombed by NATO.

Normally we're in the Ground Commander's hip pocket and we go where he goes. It works pretty good. I can go out and control air on any kind of hostile target as long as I have the Ground Commander's approval – and I don't need to have an Air Force officer present.

Yesterday, the 15th of July, I received a STEP promotion which is a Stripes for Exceptional Performance. Major General Heflebower, Commander of the 17th Air Force, came down from Ramstein and promoted me on the spot. I must say it was a joyous moment in my life. I couldn't believe it was happening to me; for a second I was thinking in a trance, my mouth just hung there, I couldn't believe I was getting a STEP promotion from the General. He had five people to promote out of eleven thousand. You just work out the odds there. Somebody was looking out for me."

# Michael Folch

### SENIOR AIRMAN, FORWARD AIR CONTROLLER, USAF

**Interviewed at Camp Demi**

"I was born on the beautiful island of Puerto Rico in 1971. Puerto Rico is a territory, a commonwealth of the United States so we're all naturalised citizens by birth. I come from the coastal village of Isabella, a small little town on the north west side of Puerto Rico. A fishing family, very ocean orientated, I've got a few brothers and sisters. I basically grew up surfing and did a little scuba diving, and a lot of octopus hunting and barracuda fishing. I worked with my grandfather a lot – fishing from small boats, we would dive for fun, spear some fish, catch some blowfish and sell them to the local people so they could mount them.

After graduating from High School I went for a while to the States to stay with my mom. Came back and was originally going to join the Coastguard but somehow I got sidetracked and ended up in the Air Force. A friend of mine, a surfer, is in the Coastguard and he said how he's always been on the coast, how he's always been able to surf; so I kind of got stoked on that situation – and all of a sudden I ended up in the Air Force.

It was pretty funny. I went to the recruiting office of the Coastguard and I was half way through the paperwork being done and I looked across the hall, and there was the Air Force recruiting office. Army, Marines, everybody. I said, 'let me look at the Air Force side of the house', and the guy basically painted a pretty picture and talked flowers into my head, telling me I would have a guaranteed job and this and that. He was more hungry to get me than the Coastguard was and I lost my composure for a moment and signed on the dotted line on the wrong side of the house. I went back to the Coastguard guy and said, 'I need my paperwork back, I'm going to the Air Force'. He was bummed out.

I came to the Air Force and after basic training volunteered for this job. It's been a very

rewarding job, very action packed, a lot of very good training. The job of Forward Air Controller is the least known career field in the Air Force, basically because we're always stationed with the Army. The Air Force doesn't like the idea of CAS (Close Air Support) because it takes away from the fighter aeroplanes. We're very lucky we're not guarding an airport or doing some admin work, or flipping hamburgers in a chow hall. We actually get job satisfaction.

The Army sees our importance in this whole thing and they reward us. There can be situations when the only assets the army can use are air. Maybe helicopters will not get there in time or they're out of range of artillery, because artillery cannot reach all the way round the world. You can get into a situation where we might be able to get aircraft in five minutes, ten minutes and the artillery or helicopters can't be moved that quickly.

Normally the Ground Commander likes to use us before anything else, they like to go 'we need air' before they even see about artillery because it's such a reliable system, the CAS, you can control the aeroplane in more detail. With artillery you're firing a bullet into the air and hoping it's going to land in the exact spot; with CAS we're double checking, triple checking, cross checking where the friendlys are, where the target is, we have eyes on the target and when an aircraft sees a target we ask him to describe it in detail.

The only thing that keeps me from going berserk is that I get a surfing magazine every month and I look back and I remember. Surfing is like a religion almost, anybody that's done it or anybody who tried to do it will tell you it's like no experience they've ever felt. It's better than sex, at the best moment's I'd say it's the best thing you can do; it's the most incredible, the most natural thing you can do, we're using the most natural resource on earth – waves, ocean energy. It doesn't give harmful by-products to the ocean, a lot of surfers help their community by trying to keep their beaches clean and fighting against the oil companies that are trying to destroy our oceans."

> The only thing that keeps me from going berserk is that I get a surfing magazine every month and I look back and I remember.

## Tyronne Kensey

### PRIVATE, 4-12 INFANTRY REGIMENT

#### Interviewed at Camp Demi

"I joined the Army because I wanted something more. I had no idea we would be coming to Bosnia but, you know, here we are doing all types of crazy things. When we first got here nobody really knew what to expect, everybody was pretty much on their toes thinking this is real combat, everybody had it in their minds, 'we're going to war, we're going to war'. After a while though everybody got real laid back, four months passed and people were like 'when are we going back'. Okay, then six months came and now this really doesn't make any sense.

There's a lot of work to be done but I think the Army are the wrong people to do it. They gave us a mission and when we got here they changed it and I don't think that was right. On all the briefings that we had they said we would come here and it was going to be war and we were going to have to keep our heads down; and then when we got here all

we were doing was filling sandbags and building bunkers and walking around saying 'Hello' to everyone, that was pretty much it. I was expecting what they had told us – war. I was expecting to get off the plane and run to the bunker and lock in low from that point on. I was more excited than scared. When you join the military, that's what you think – war. Of course you're going to have to go one day and we were just, I'm not going to say hoping, waiting for that moment to come.

I think America should pack up and go back to their home stations because our mission is done here, there's nothing left to do. We'll let the city police and the MPs handle the rest. There's a lot of political demonstrations but other than that nobody wants to start anything. If they can go a whole year without fighting I think they're going to say, 'Well, if we can go a whole year then there's no need to fight at all.'

The Army is great. You work for all types of different people. Most of the time the lower enlisted really don't agree with the higher up people, you know, officers and high NCOs (Non Commissioned Officers), because some of the decisions they make really don't make any sense at all. But the military is all about following orders and I guess that's just what we've got to do, it gets really difficult but it's out of respect for the people. We'll do it and complain later. Some officers and some high NCOs want a good report on their name so they make you do the stupid stuff – to make them look good, that's what I don't think is right. I believe if the Army goes back to the NCO creed – which says Mission, Men, Myself – I think we'd all get along much better. The top priority is the mission, you want to get the job done, the second is taking care of my men, and the last thing an NCO should think about is himself.

> **I think America should pack up and go back to their home stations because our mission is done here, there's nothing left to do.**

Bosnia is great but I wish I was here not in the military. I think we'll have to go to Budapest on a road trip, where we can get out and really mingle with the people. Right now we're locked down on post and we can't speak to different people, so we can't know what's on their minds. Some of the women look really good. The UN has a different mentality as far as looking after people is concerned. IFOR is all about going in there and 'we're going to hit them hard, we're going to be big and bad', but when we go up to it and get face to face with the monster it's, 'Oh, we're going to back down now. Everyone leave.'

The UN went in there not to be bullies but to show that we have that presence, we have that force, that's what it's all about. The IFOR talk a good game but they can't really play a good game. For IFOR to be really busy they would have to be pushed a very long way, like a person who doesn't have a bad temper, you keep on messing with him, keep on messing but if you push him too hard he will break. Everybody is waiting because in the back of everyone's mind is 'something will happen', everybody has that in the back of their minds. The Army has an old saying, 'stay alert, stay alive', and pretty much everyone goes by that.

There are a lot of families that believe we're here for no good reason, a lot of families believe, 'Why do I have to send my son, or husband, or wife over to a country that we have nothing to do with'. If the US loses one person here it will be a political disaster because basically we're here for no good reason.

If I could do all this again I probably wouldn't have volunteered to come out here. The UN and IFOR are two different sides of the same coin, I would work for the UN again, but IFOR . . . I've done it, I did it and that's about all I can say about them."

Top.
Privates Corey Causey on left and Tyronne Kensey on right take a break during a bunker blowing mission in the hills above Kladanj.

Bottom.
Tyronne Kensey with M16 rifle takes a break from a bunker blowing mission in the hills above Kladanj.

# Corey Causey

## PRIVATE, 4-12 INFANTRY REGIMENT

### Interviewed at Camp Demi

"I'm from Chicago, Illinois, and I joined the Army for a lot of different reasons, the main one being I was getting tired of a lot of monotonous jobs. Doing nothing, going nowhere and, I guess, for the adventure of it.

I think the US should not have been here so early; everything was jumped through hoops to get here and I believe that was partly because the UN was not taking a more active role in this war. Humanitarian aid is good but if bullets are flying down the range at you, I would have taken a more active role. Army life is giving. You can't say exactly what you put into it is what you get back because some put more into it and get back less than others. It could be better, a lot better. Too many things are glorified, whereas day to day activities, such as coming back from patrol without casualties, needs to be highlighted a little bit more. What I can see is that everyone in this unit is glory hungry, just so hungry for a tab or something glorious to go back with.

I've seen a lot of intimidation done on our part, like the recent demonstration on the Serb side when we were put on a high security level – but we just backed down. It really wasn't like you read in the papers, the military filters down what they want you to hear. Some of the threats made by our highers are just facetious.

Being in the infantry you get shafted, you do what everyone else doesn't want to do, while you get the fat butts up in Tuzla sucking back the benefits of your hard labour. We run a checkpoint out here that really isn't our focal, it could be done better by a Military Police Unit. Also, we helped construct the checkpoint from the ground level – I'll remember that day. It could've been done by the engineers but of course they find all sorts of excuses why they can't come out and do missions. No one really looks out for us, nobody seems to say, 'Hey, that really isn't those guys' job'. We're already getting dogged from doing patrols, dreary tired, four hours on shift, six hours down, ready at any time to join a Quick Reaction Force.

The mission here in Bosnia? Since the second month we were here, February, I can't see any purpose for us being out here. Military Police, yeah, working closely with the UN and the UN taking a more active role. The UN just dropped the ball. Obviously Serbia and the warring factions did not take the UN seriously. This camp here was just an onion and potato field when we first came. We slept close to ninety days in tents, in the dead of winter. It wasn't as bad as Chicago but the Army equipment they issued to us was, I'm not going to lie, sub-standard. I myself came very close to frostbite. I know some of my comrades did get frostbite. Not too much consideration was given to the soldiers during the patrolling, walking the ZOS, checking to see if areas were clear of mines. We even lost a battalion commander's truck – his Bradley ran over a mine, we thought it was a cleared area. We've even walked through minefields.

The NCOs we work directly with try and do as much as they can but, at the same time, they're afraid of catching heat rounds for us. The senior NCOs are just out to please commanders and commanders are always trying to cheese up to higher colonels and generals, it just rolls uphill. The UN has better benefits. Our mission in Macedonia was to be highly visible; we were doing border patrols, actually walking along the Serbian border. More dangerous, but at the same time not, than this mission. We didn't have the support we needed right there, we were all self sufficient. It was a lot better with the UN,

not all these strings tied behind your back. In Macedonia we were allowed to mingle with the people, you could go into the capital Skopje and get to know the culture a lot better. Here, none of that's going on.

The US is spending funds here, a lot, but not for the right reasons. I don't want to take anything away from the dining facility but I'm sure a lot of money went into that work. Here, we have a hard time getting a T-850 which is the equipment we use. I know my equipment has needed to be turned in since we got out here and I think it's more important to have equipment that works than a full belly. I can go a day without eating, but I'd rather have equipment that works."

# Radmillo Pantic

## TRANSLATOR WITH 4-12 INFANTRY

### Interviewed at Camp Demi

"I was born in Serbia in the city of Loznica, 25 kilometres away from the city I have lived most of my life in – Zvornik – on the Bosnian Serb side. I liked Yugoslavia, the former Yugoslavia that we all lived in, we had a decent life, I had my good friends. When war started I lost most of my friends. Some of them left, a lot of them died. The people who I lived with in my town were mostly Muslim, so most of my friends were Muslim. So now I ain't got no other friends except my buddy Ed here (a Muslim translator) and IFOR soldiers in Alpha Company that I work for now.

I have been a soldier in the war, Military Police. It was tough. I've been wounded once in a battle. Soldiers don't like war. I blame politicians for all of this, for the atrocities, war crimes. A lot of people died, mostly on the Muslim side, they died on the Serb side too, but we have to be realistic and we have to admit that one side suffered more than the other in the war. On the 8th of October 1992, I lost six members of my family, my relatives, they were slaughtered. But I ain't going to blame nobody else but politicians and if it was up to me a lot more people, the political people in charge on all three sides, would appear at the court in the Hague.

Before, all of us were faced towards the west. We liked English music, we liked American music, the American way of life and we thought all was going to be good. Young people are not guilty, the older people, the politicians, are guilty for this war. They made the wrong decisions, they should have said 'the people want to live together, let it be that way.' Everybody knew we could not create 'Big Serbia' or 'Big Croatia' and tear Bosnia apart, it ain't going to happen.

We need more than one year to create a democratic government and a democratic society because you cannot make a democratic government overnight. It takes several generations to do that. The thing is, we must put the right people in charge, not the nationalists, the people who think only about themselves, how to make more money, how to stay in charge. We have to think about the next generation, we cannot think about what was before, we have to think about what will be in the future.

The situation that I live in is now very difficult. I don't think I can stay here; I think I'm going to move to the States but, if it's going to work, I might come back here in the future. Some people on the Serb side see me being an interpreter for IFOR as bad, and some of them think that I am a traitor. It's probably jealousy, because I'm making some

money now. Because of the media the Serbs think the Americans came here to support one side. I cannot say this is true but it looks like they are supporting the Bosnian Army to be as strong as the Serbian Army.

Some people use this war to earn a lot of money. On the Serbian side the regime is like a Communist regime in the Soviet Union in the time of Stalin. If you want to open a shop, a grocery store, you have to become a member of the SDS (Serb Democratic Party) like my cousin had to do. If you don't want to be a member you're going to be a fugitive, like I am. Right now I don't see a future on the Serb side if the SDS stay in charge. Some people support them but at the elections they are going to lose. That's my opinion because ordinary people aren't going to support them in my city or in Banja Luka. We had four years of war, four years of suffering, four years of embargo.

It's not that good to see the news – SKY or CNN – and see everybody say 'Serbs are wrong'. You cannot then say 'everybody is wrong and I am good', you have to face the facts that the Serbs committed some crimes. What happened in Tuzla on the 25th May 1995, that's bad, or what happened in Sarajevo or what happened about the fall of Srebrenica last year, seven thousand people suddenly disappeared. The thing about mass graves and atrocities and what the Serbs did to the Muslim people and what the Croats did to the Muslim people, and what the Muslims did to the Serb people in Bosnia – that's bad.

When the Serbs were shelling Tuzla on May 25th last year, seventy one people died in a place called 'the gate'. I saw the pictures and I saw the movie about it. There were helpless people lying on the ground, many of them dead, wounded, screaming for help. I saw the same pictures on the Serb side, and that's the bad part; we're going to have, in our memories, bad pictures about war because there ain't no good pictures about war. My friend died in the war, my best friend. I'm going to remember those pictures, you can't just delete them from your memory. Even when we're talking about girls, football, about anything, it always ends up on war.

Nothing changed between me and my friend, my best friend, a Muslim, even though we didn't see each other for four and a half years. He never said a bad word about me, he lost his father in the war, he lost his house, he's been wounded three times. When I was on the frontline the only thing I thought about was not to see him on the other side.

It's hard to explain; it's so difficult. Once you had a life, a good life, and all of a sudden it changed. You ain't got no house, no friends, no money and you ain't got no happiness. I'm proud to be an Orthodox Serb, but not with the Serbs who are in charge now, because a lot of bad things happened in my city at the beginning of the war and during the war. It's not my city no more, even the buildings are not the same. The city had his own spirit, his own way of life, we had our places where we gathered. Now, the people who live there are refugees, but I don't know them, it's not my city no more.

We lived together before the war and we did good, we had one Yugoslavia, we were recognised in the world, I had my passport, I could travel all round the world and if someone asked me 'Where are you from?' then I would say 'Yugoslavia', and everybody would say 'You're cool'. Right now I can go to Hungary and that's it, because I need a visa to see my sister in Austria or my brother in Germany. That's bad. But I think by the time the wounds heal it's going to be much better.

Young people and educated people think like I do. The bad thing is that there are a lot of people thinking about Serbian pride or united Big Serbia, Great Serbia, about what happened seven or eight centuries ago when Serbia was an empire. It's like an Englishman thinking about the United States as a part of Great Britain. The young people are faced towards the west. They think about progress, about how to make money, how to

Top.
Radmilo Pantic, a Serb translator at Camp Demi known as 'Iceman', on the left with 'Ed', a Muslim translator called Behrem Adnan. Although Serbs and Muslims are thought to always hate one another, these two are the best of friends.

Bottom.
Members of 4-12 Infantry in formation for daily physical exercise routine, Camp Demi.

have more fun and how to live together. I don't see any advantage of Great Serbia; you have France, Germany, UK and USA with millions of Muslim people. If you're not recognised by the other countries you're a loser.

There was a time when I thought all of them were wrong – I'm good, I'm proud to be a Serb. I am a Serb, I am an Orthodox Christian and I believe in God, but we have to be realistic. There are people who know that the Serbs have to face the facts; that we cannot live separately, we have to live together again, all of us.

There's a big difference between the UN forces and IFOR. UN forces were here to help the people, IFOR is here to enforce the peace. They have every right to shoot back if someone shoots at them, they have the firepower. But I think that if there were no American soldiers here it would be the same situation as UNPROFOR.

When I was a soldier we had a situation in Zvornik; we stopped two UN transporters, they called me to translate because I was the only one who spoke English. I opened the door of the transporter and it was General Morillon. He was scared to death. There was a riot, maybe two or three hundred people around the transporter, they were yelling. I know he earned a medal of honour but he was scared that day. He told me twenty times, 'Your duty is to protect me'. The radical Serbs were there, I'm talking about the Chetnicks, they had knives in their hands and they showed him how they were going to cut his throat. All of us knew it wasn't going to happen, we had the situation under control, but they made a bad picture about Serbs in General Morillon's eyes. We could do whatever we wanted with the UN forces.

The big difference with IFOR is that there ain't going to be a war. If IFOR was here before, in Srebrenica, nobody would have died; Serbs just took over, in front of UN forces. The Americans are the ones who had to break the ice, to say, 'Stop – this is enough, it's the end'. That's good. Some people on both sides think IFOR shouldn't be here, but they had to come here, they had to, because I wonder how many more people would have to die. The bad part about war is the loss of so many young lives in our culture. It's going to take a while to recover. Those people who died in war, my friends, his friends, we ain't going to bring them back from death.

From my point of view IFOR is cool. I met a lot of friends and they introduced me to the American way of life and the American Army way of life. The bad thing is that they're going to leave at the end of the year, but I think they're going to stay. If they leave there's going to be another war, definitely.

The war in this territory will stop finally, for ever, when all the people here understand that we are, in fact, one nation, one Bosnian nation with different religions. We have Bosnian Serbs, Bosnian Croats, Bosnian Muslims – but we are all Bosnians and Bosnia was my country, Bosnia was his country and we had seven million Bosnians before the war. We lived together. I don't see the reason why we can't live together in the future."

## THE TURKISH BRIGADE

# Ahmet Berberoglu

COLONEL, COMMANDER, TURKISH BRIGADE

### Interviewed in Turkish HQ, Zenica

"We have been in NATO since 1952 and we have become accustomed to the Americans. They have helped us a lot and we are very happy to work under them. General Nash is, to me, like a Rambo with brains.

Under the UN flag the Turkish were a Task Force organisation, but after transferring to IFOR we were reinforced and have been upgraded to Brigade level. We are very happy to be in this country; we have historical links and, as part of our national policy, as there had been some pressure in our country, we had to be here to try and help bring peace.

Historically we were the dominant power in this area for four hundred years and during the nineteenth century we had to withdraw from this area, the Balkans, back to Turkey. As a result of this withdrawal some people had to emigrate from Bosnia, back to Turkey – more than four million people. They are in a very healthy position now, they use their mother language and have full rights of Turkish citizenship. Their children are serving in the Turkish Army and the government sector. We have some Bosniaks in this unit.

Zenica is a dominantly Bosniak (Bosnian Muslim) area; about eighty two per cent are Bosniak, fourteen or fifteen per cent are Croat and the others are Serb. The three communities are living together in peace and the three communities are represented in the Mayor's assembly. In the beginning there was some fighting in and around Zenica but now everyone is trying to keep the peace here.

At the beginning of the war some Mujahadeen and religious groups came to Zenica and established a training camp here. After the Dayton agreement most of them have been withdrawn and sent back to their countries or somewhere else in the world. But some of them got married to local people and got the right to citizenship, maybe twenty or thirty. It has been declared by the United States Government that there is no link between Iranian Military Intelligence and the Bosnian government and therefore the Equip and Train programme will start. One of the pre-conditions was that all foreign forces should be withdrawn.

As an IFOR unit we do not have any responsibilities for implementing this programme, but Turkey, in a bilateral programme, has begun training a tank company and an artillery battery. The first phase will be completed at the beginning of August.

The belief of Islam by the Bosniaks is a modern understanding, a modern approach of Islam and I wish they will preserve what they practise now. There are some foreign ideas and propaganda campaigns that Bosniaks are invited to a different type of Islamic belief – this would be very, very dangerous for them, it will be very, very dangerous for their future. There are some propaganda campaigns by some other Islamic countries other than Turkey that are trying to shift their path to other ways. I don't want to see Bosniaks going different ways, I want them to be in the way they practise now. For the moment they are very moderate, very calm in their beliefs, their understanding is a more civilised Islamic belief. Clothing, for example – most of them wear western clothes whereas in most Islamic

The image at top right is the "IFOR on IFOR" logo.countries you will see a different type of clothing. It's a detailed point. They have great amounts of tolerance to other beliefs, they are ready to live together with Catholics and Orthodox.

For the moment, most of the people want to live together, even if they have different cultures, different beliefs or different ethnic groups. The Bosnian Government wants to create a democratic state which is multi-ethnic, multi-national and multi-belief. All social groups once had tolerance towards each other, especially in belief and culture, and if they reached this level then it would be easy to live together.

I don't believe IFOR will leave Bosnia at the end of December. Maybe there will be some restructuring of troops in Theatre, maybe some lightly equipped units will remain to monitor the peace accord. If other nations stay here, we will stay with them since we want to be together with other NATO troops. Before IFOR everyone had observed that every peace accord, every ceasefire, will not be effective without American troops. Turkey will not act unilaterally here. Turkey wants to be in any conflict as a global partner. We want to be together with other nationalities."

# Ali Hakan Kete

## LIEUTENANT, BASED AT HQ, TURKISH BRIGADE

### Interviewed outside Zenica Steelworks

"This is the second biggest steelworks in Europe, the biggest is in Poland. It was closed during the war because it was a target for Serb artillery. In June 1996 two sections of it were opened and President Izetbegovic was at the opening ceremony. Zenica was one of the most quiet areas during the war, that's why it became a centre for trade. They had a chance economically during the war.

I think this factory will be important for Bosnia in the future; but this is only a factory, the material is coming from the other side, the Serbian side. In the former Yugoslavia there were three parts to producing anything: the raw materials came from the Serbian side, it was manufactured in Bosnia and exported from Croatia. That was the Communist system: one of them has the material, one has the factory and one has the way out. I think there is a chance again, if this peace process goes on successfully. They have to co-operate and I think they are ready to. There is no way out for Bosnia-Herzegovina if they don't co-operate with Croatia and Serbia.

Hatred is the most easy thing to keep. You can give up your love easily but you can't give up your hate too easily. They just need time I think. In Bosnia-Herzegovina the hate is not seen on the main media, they're not exaggerating it. Here the media is quite independent. I have no information about the Serb media. We make some radio programmes and some radio shows and we make video clips on Turkish pop music.

It is interesting how all three communities in Zenica have really good relations. As far as we know there was only one incident of Croat nationalism in Zenica in 1994 and after that there was no fighting. After the Turkish forces came there were no incidents and we tried our best to keep relations between the three communities alive. We repaired the Orthodox church, the Catholic church and the Mosque and there was no reaction, they were all happy. Some of the opening ceremonies, for example at the Orthodox church, were attended by the Muslim clergy."

Opposite, top.
Turkish Quick Reaction Force on a practise alert at their Brigade HQ in Zenica.

Bottom left.
Colonel Ahmet Berberoglu, Commander of the Turkish Brigade, in his office at the steelworks in Zenica.

Bottom right.
Turkish soldiers during an exercise at their Brigade HQ in Zenica

Overleaf, left hand page.

Top.
Lieutenant Ali Hakan Kete, the Turkish Brigade Media Officer, talking in English at the Brigade HQ. Note the sun breaking through the storm clouds in the mountains behind.

Bottom.
Turkish soldiers take cover among the long grass that has overgrown the disused railway line at Zenica Steelworks.

Right hand page.
Top.
Turkish machine gunners take up defensive positions outside their Brigade HQ, Zenica steelworks.

Bottom.
Zenica: view of the second largest steelworks in Europe, now overgrown and home to the Turkish and Romanian Brigades.

## THE NORDIC-POLISH BRIGADE

## Marek Stawecki

PRIVATE, BMP DRIVER (ARMOURED PERSONNEL DRIVER)
POLISH BATTALION

### Interviewed at Polish HQ

"I'm from the Tarnow region in southern Poland. I enlisted in the Army and went to the BMP driver's school – five and a half months, with a lot of exercises and strange conditions. In my opinion, the BMP is easier to drive than a car. In the beginning it was hard but when you feel it, it's not a problem. It's comfortable, quick and very manoeuvrable, it's better than the American Bradley which is too high and easy to hit with anti-tank guns.

I volunteered to come down to Bosnia. I wondered how it was and I wanted to test myself, also to get some money."

## Janek Wxsocki

PPRIVATE, QRF (QUICK REACTION FORCE) POLISH BATTALION

### Interviewed at Polish HQ

"The American Army is full of electronics and computer equipment, but it's not shooting itself, you need a man. I believe that we test ourselves in war conditions, in action. It's mainly a question of men. I'm quite sure we're good soldiers.

It's like computers. You can have hardware but without software it's not working. We are the software and I believe we are compatible. I am a gunner, a good gunner, and I appreciate my education in this military business. I was five and a half months in specialist school; it was not so hard. We have a good commander, a really clever guy, he can get through to us, we understand him, we feel him.  Also, we feel as a team in this BMP.

When I was in Military School it was simple, but here we are driving through mountains so now I'm gaining great experience and am getting to the maximum of my skills.  In Poland we don't have these conditions. When we were on patrol we were looking for a suspected Mujahadeen camp. We weren't sure where we were going and it was almost like war conditions."

## Piotr Krol

PRIVATE, POLISH BATTALION

### Interviewed at Polish HQ

"My training was tough but I think clever. I feel that it helped me, particularly the marches of twenty to fifty kilometres. I feel I can pass everything. I had to jump and shoot

Top left.
Piotr Krol, member of Polish
Quick Reaction
Force being interviewed at
the Polish Brigade HQ.

Top right.
Marek Stawecki, member
of the Polish Quick
Reaction Force being
interviewed at the Polish HQ.

Bottom.
Jacek Wxsocki, driver of BMP-1
Armoured Peronnel Carrier,
being interviewed at HQ.

and I'm a good shot. The gym helped me to keep my condition and be manoeuvrable. I feel the power. We were specially trained in martial arts, mixed martial arts, unarmed defence, and to kill in silence if we need to.

The situation was tense here, but it has decreased and we feel much more secure than we did when we arrived. When we arrived, what surprised us were the buildings – how they were destroyed in one part but fine in another. We thought Bosnia was totally destroyed.

We feel great support from the other Armies. We can give some support but we feel support with their technology. There's the Danes with their tanks, their Leopards can come here and support us; also the Americans with their choppers. When there was an accident they came very quickly and helped us to withdraw from the minefield. The Norwegians on the SISU (Finnish made APC) medical evacuation team also came very quickly to help our guys. We basically feel very secure having the support of the other units."

# Tuevo Tikkanen

MAJOR, FINNISH BATTALION
PRESS AND INFORMATION OFFICE

**Interviewed at Nordic-Polish Brigade HQ, Doboj**

"One of our tasks is to have relations with local media. We have two sides – Federation and Serbian – and we have weekly meetings with both of them. Relations are good and we are planning a direct phone-in show with Radio Doboj. We must remember that during the war newspapers and radios were totally the tools of the warring parties. Radio Doboj had twenty four hour programming and the war is over now but they say the war is not over.

In a way the tension in this area is depending on the media, and the state and authorities totally use the media. Is this democratic? I don't know, but I do know that this is very hard compared to the Middle East where the situation I saw was also very hard. We try to be active and not reactive, we try to tell positive news about positive things we have done. We have lent generators to the city; we have repaired roads. I think it is important to inform people in practical matters, not tell them about Sweden or Finland.

The News Editor of Radio Doboj told us we should know how people think about IFOR. She told us IFOR had killed seventeen persons in traffic accidents. This is not true. Then she said that IFOR has occupied their country and they want IFOR to leave very soon, but what happens then? They complain about the roads and say IFOR is the reason for bad roads! Our main task is to inform people and to have the right information, to be frank and fair. Public relations is a very difficult area but the beginning is to tell the truth.

Finnish soldiers have very long experience in UN missions. We have just celebrated forty years of UN peace-keeping duties. Finnish soldiers think they have a good military background; their fathers were in the Winter War with Russia from 1939 to 1945, so why should we not be good ? They have a strong feeling that they are not Red Cross soldiers, but we are real soldiers. In this mission it is the Finnish Construction Battalion and they have experts. In this NATO mission we think Finnish soldiers have much to give.

Top.
Polish soldiers of
the Quick Reaction Force
practise an alert.

Bottom.
Polish soldiers in full battle
dress in front of their
BMP-1 Armoured Personnel
Carrier.

In 1939 the Russians attacked Finland and our Army was in very poor condition. We had a Civil War in 1918 and the parties were separated, but at the beginning of the war Finland had totally united and everyone thought we should forget our differences. This war was very hard and many European countries were invaded – Norway and Denmark were occupied. About one hundred thousand Finnish soldiers were killed but Finland was never invaded.

Our estimate is that maybe six hundred thousand Russian soldiers were killed in this war, maybe more, some estimates are of one million dead. We developed special tactics in the forest where we let their forces come in, surround them, ambush them and gradually defeat them. We could use winter conditions very well, we would hide in the snow and use the darkness. The Russians became afraid of the dark and of the snow. Finnish guerrillas had skis and they went far away in small groups to attack the Russians. We had some weapons but the Russians had a hundred times more artillery and tanks than us. It is a story about success although we lost very much."

## Transcript from Serb Radio Doboj

Interview with Jovanka Petrovic,
an old lady living in the Doboj suburb of Usora. July 1996

JOVANKA PETROVIC: ". . . I want to curse each Serb who believes in Muslims – I hope he will not see any member of his family alive if he does. Each brother Serb who does it and trusts Muslims deserves such kind of punishment. That is my message. . ."

RADIO DOBOJ SPOKESMAN: ". . . let this be a warning for other Serbs in Doboj and in the whole area of Republika Srpska, so they can see how it would look like to live together with enemies who have been our enemies and cut-throats for centuries . . . The citizens of Doboj de-facto do not trust anybody. They can even less trust the Implementation Force which we are calling IFOR. The reason for that is extreme partiality, if we are talking about the former warring factions. The Latin people are famous swindlers, and Muslims with Islam religion are perfidious. The IFOR members are both of that at the same time. While the representatives from Doboj and Tesanj municipalities are trying to find solutions to the problems concerning the freedom of movement, as well as for other actual problems, the 'world peace-keepers' (how they call themselves) have their own plans, and basically these plans are made with only one side – the Muslim side. That is the reason why their activities and actions are synchronised . . ."

## Soren Bruun Rasmussen

### CAPTAIN, DANISH BATTALION

#### Interviewed at Danish base, Doboj

"The Danish Battalion has four companies: Infantry, Logistics, Tank and Headquarters. There's been a lot of movement at the Azura Bridge and unfortunately they try to do it in larger groups and this leads to trouble. If more than twenty people from the Muslim side

Top.
Propaganda for a radical Serbian political party led by the notorious Arkan, an assassin, war criminal, Mafia boss and member of the Serbian Parliament. Arkan's Radical Party advocates ethnic purity and the driving out of all Muslim or Croat inhabitants of the so-called 'historic Serb lands'. The posters are displayed on a road sign by a gutted Muslim house near Doboj.

Bottom.
Poster of Serbian indicted war criminal Radovan Karadzic, pasted onto a road sign in Doboj. Although Karadzic has been barred from public office by the Dayton Accord, his passion for ethnic hatred continues to strongly influence the controlled state media and consequently the Serb people in Bosnia.

try to cross the bridge, the Serbs on the Doboj side will gather and try and stop them from visiting their homes. It's not a Border but it's like a Border. I can't see the situation improving because there's too much hate between the groups. It's only possible to keep the peace if you keep the Muslims in one area and the Serbs in another.

There was an incident when a rifleman shot at me. He was probably drunk and he missed me by five or ten metres; he had shot from a block of flats so I could not shoot back. My family think it's okay me being here because it's my job. I think we are doing some good here but I also know that when we leave things will go bad again."

# Kjell Nordlie

## DOCTOR, NORDIC MEDICAL COMPANY, TUZLA.

### Interviewed at 'Blue Factory' Hospital Facility, Tuzla

"I'm from Oslo and I've worked all over Norway. I had no connection with the Army, except when I came here, to do something I have wanted to do all my life. I came here in mid-April 1994. As a young medical student I was always dreaming of going out in the world and doing something, but then you get family, you have to try and make a career which I made – sort of. But in the end, after what was like thirty years in prison, I chose to break out.

This work with the refugees gives me such happiness. Every time I have been out in the refugee camps, and that has been almost every day, I have such a good feeling because I have done something, not much, but what I can. It's much more interesting to do all kinds of work here than being a heart specialist in Norway.

I have seen a lot of nasty things, really nasty things. I was here when that massacre in Tuzla happened, on the 25th of May, 1995, when a lot of people were killed and lot of people were injured. It made a great impression on me. The first things we were asked for by the local hospital were for plastic bags for arms and legs that had been torn off. That was terrible, really terrible.

I have become sort of an old man. I am fifty eight now. I am too old to be one of those doctors who goes out in rescue teams and things like that. I must know my place which is as an internist and as a microbiologist here, and also as a doctor for refugees. I am very busy receiving IFOR soldiers in the reception all morning, and after lunch I get out into the refugee camps where I work for three, four, five hours, coming back in time for a late dinner. After that I am usually on duty again, because there are so few doctors here. It has happened that I am on duty for twenty four hours a day.

We have seen nasty examples of mine accidents, terrible things. I have seen several young soldiers with damaged legs which had to be amputated, terrible head injuries, belly wounds. I think a lot of things we see would make many people faint, for example when you see a bad head injury and the brain comes out of the skull – that's a nasty sight.

There have been maybe twenty mine injuries here, all after the cease-fire because, before that people couldn't go out into the fields. But now people start to look for mines, and there are many who are not experienced in this search for mines and they just step on mine traps.

As an internist I am used to taking care of people with heart attacks, I am used to seeing people dying, that is normal, but usually that is with old people. But here you see

Top.
UN international policemen pose for photographs by a burned out Serb T-55 tank and BVP carrier, near Doboj.

Bottom left.
Dr Kjel Nordlie, a Norwegian doctor at the 'Blue Factory' medical facility near Tuzla. Dr Nordlie spends a lot of time running clinics for refugees, thousands of whom live in collective centres around Tuzla.

Bottom right.
Tuevo Tikkannen, a Finnish media monitoring officer with the Nordic-Polish Brigade, relaxes at Brigade HQ in Doboj.

IFOR
on
IFOR

those young soldiers being injured and killed by those mines. Before the ceasefire we had a lot of shelling. We had quite a lot of soldiers from the UN who were hit by shrapnel, quite a lot of bad things.

To be frank, I think UN was more popular than IFOR. Though there has been a ceasefire for more than half a year now, they take more precautions now, especially the Americans. I suppose because they have been to war in so many places in the world – Vietnam, Africa, the Middle East – they are strict about all kinds of rules. American soldiers, even in the worst heat in this country, have to wear all their equipment, flak-jacket, helmet, all kinds of equipment, sweating like hell. Some of these ideas have been transmitted to the other nations so we have stricter rules than we had during the real war.

In the beginning of the IFOR period we had quite a lot of trouble with the Americans because they refused to take Norwegian doctors or nurses in their helicopters; there were a couple of months when that was forbidden. We had quite a lot of struggle to solve that problem; it was insurance: 'we will be sued', political. It is much better now, it is okay, but it took some time.

I think I have had about thirteen thousand refugee patients during the last two and a half years. They come from all over Bosnia, mostly from the countryside and small villages. I must say I am absolutely not a racist, and don't feel like a superior person or anything like that, but it's a fact that these people are extremely ignorant. They know nothing about history, nothing about geography, nothing about other cultures – and they are very religious.

Out in the countryside, because of old traditions, there is a lot of in-breeding, which is definitely not good. But, I cannot say that those people are less intelligent than people from the city. I have no proof of that. The problem is they never got any kind of education, that's the big difference. After fifty years of Communism, everybody in former Yugoslavia should be entitled to have education, free, but they haven't got it and, because of old traditions, and very much due to religion, the women are something inferior, they're not allowed to go to school.

I have had many strange experiences with these patients. For example it's almost impossible to get one of those refugee women to take off her blouse to examine her heart because it's shameful to show her breasts. It's even difficult to take off the scarf on their heads because men are not supposed to see their hair, so there are many strange things here. They are so superstitious that you can make them believe anything practically.

I think religion is the main cause of the war. I hate to talk about politics but I can say, quite frankly, I hate religions, I cannot stand religion. I think that it is one of the worst things ever invented by mankind. Man can never agree about what kind of imaginary God they shall believe in. Personally I don't believe in any God, any devils, any saints, any prophets. I just love to help those suffering people.

There will be enormous problems for decades. It will take twenty years to rebuild all those damaged cities, everywhere, even in small villages you see bullet holes, marks after grenades, and so many refugees. It will be an immense problem for many, many years.

I see psychological problems when I am out in the Refugee Camps, in that little 'Ambulanta' as we call it, where I sit to receive patients. One of the usual things I see is crying women – they have lost husbands, children. I have heard so many stories of women who have actually seen their family, their male members of the family, being shot before their eyes, by the enemy. So, of course, there are a lot of psychological problems. I am very restrictive in giving out nerve medicines, I don't like them. Psychosomatic problems are big here – headaches, palpitations, shivering. These are some of the most usual symptoms I deal with.

Top.
Patrick O'Reilly Molholm, a former member of the Royal Irish Rangers and now a Norwegian Army Officer and Operational Officer at the 'Blue Factory' medical facility outside Tuzla. Note the hat for the Royal Irish Rangers on the right and the Norwegian flag on his arm.

Bottom.
Scandanavian and American troops doing fitness exercises outside the 'Blue Factory' medical facility near Tuzla. Note the Finnish-made SISU armoured ambulances in the background.

I will stay here as long as is possible, as long as I am allowed to stay. You could say I have come to love these people. It will be very hard to leave because I know for sure the local health system does not work for these people. They consider the refugees sort of shit, I know it."

# Patrick O'Reilly Molholm

LIEUTENANT, NORWEGIAN MEDICAL COMPANY

**Interviewed at 'Blue Factory' hospital facility, near Tuzla**

"My job at the moment is Operations Officer – 'OpsOff'. We sit in the ops room and basically if a medevac happens we go out and get them. Normally we get one or two accidents a day, everything from mine to road traffic accidents. The last person who was dead was a Muslim who got electrocuted. The family came and took him away.

I was born in the south of England because my dad was in the Royal Navy, although my mother was Norwegian. I went to boarding school at the age of nine, outside Ipswich, and then I went to a Navy boarding school from the age of eleven. I dropped out at fourteen, I didn't get on, I didn't enjoy it, and then I moved to London and went to a normal Comprehensive School. I left school at sixteen with a couple of O levels and joined the Army at seventeen and a half. My mum's and my dad's side of the family are all military.

> In the Norwegian Army, the only thing I'd say it's got going for it is bloody good pay – it's good money, and an easy life – it's like a holiday.

I initially wanted the Royal Marines but I failed the medical. I joined the Royal Irish Rangers – my grand-dad was in the London Irish Rifles during the war. I actually wanted the Irish Hussars, which is a tank regiment, but when I got to Sutton Coldfield, which is the recruitment and selection centre, they told me the Hussars were full up and I could have the Rangers if I wanted. I felt I was personally conned – I heard later if I had just stuck to my guns and said, 'No, it's the Hussars or nothing', I'd have probably got it. But, looking back on it, I've no regrets. I'm proud of having been in the Rangers.

We were posted to Berlin, then the Falklands, Belize, Kenya, Canada for big exercises and I've also been to Northern Ireland. I'm not so sure it's an advantage to have military experience from the British Army being in the Norwegian Army because the Norwegian's are so much more relaxed, and they're not really a fighting force. Sometimes I think the Norwegians think I am too military.

The Norwegian Army is ideal for supporting others, for coming in to a UN or a NATO mission with hospitals or logistics, the rear echelon. They're good at supporting, they couldn't come with infantry or tanks. They have infantry. They're trying to put together a battalion that is earmarked to go abroad, but they're having problems filling up just one battalion. In Norway, it's only sergeants and above who are in for more than one year, everyone else is a national serviceman, only in for twelve months.

If you could get a combination, somewhere in the middle, between the British Army on the one extreme and the Norwegians on the other, if you could get something there in the middle, then I think you might be able to get the perfect army. The British Army is maybe a bit too strict, has too much of a social class barrier, too much bang your heels

together and 'Yes sir', follow orders, whereas in the Norwegian Army you get called into a union meeting and asked to explain why you made one order. You'll get privates coming into the ops room saying, 'What the bloody hell did you call me in here for.' This can be classed, by an ex-Brit like myself, as very disrespectful.

The civilian society is reflected by its military. In Britain you wouldn't want to go out and have a drink on your own, you'd want a mate or two to look after you and cover your back. Britain is quite aggressive and it reflects in its Army as well – the boys are tough. Whereas in Norway they're a bit more laid back and this reflects in their Army as well.

I would say, for doing the job, the British Infantry is the best in the world. I would rate them higher than the Americans. If Norway was invaded, I think you would see a completely different Norwegian soldier, but as it is at the moment they're not a fighting man.

For job satisfaction I felt I was a better soldier in the Royal Irish Rangers, it's a better unit. The comradeship was outstanding, a small group of friends, the family feeling, you're in a regiment with 350 years of tradition. In the Norwegian Army, the only thing I'd say it's got going for it is bloody good pay – it's good money, and an easy life – it's like a holiday. For me, it's purely financial. I'm married now, to a Norwegian girl."

# The British Division

# Dominic Roberts

## 2ND LIEUTENANT, 1ST DRAGOON GUARDS

### Interviewed in Challenger tank near Sipovo

"I'm out here with my troop of three Challenger main battle tanks and two Scimitar reconnaissance vehicles for use on patrol in this area. We've been out here for two weeks now. I'm very proud, very lucky to be out here, bringing my tanks out. People don't really think you can use tanks in this sort of operation.

Tanks work extremely well out here and all the fears about not being able to use the routes and go up into the hills were completely wrong. They managed to take the tanks anywhere all the other vehicles could go. For the two Scimitar light recce vehicles this terrain is perfect, there's nowhere they can't go and, in the few places where the tanks are a little bit big for the tracks in the hills, the Scimitars do the job perfectly for us.

At the moment my squadron is based in Mrkonic Grad and we are on a rotation; what happens is that we go out to some troop outposts in the country and we'll operate there, bring the twelve guys for about a week at a time. We provide checkpoints on the road, patrol the area providing the security so that freedom of movement can exist; a Croat, a Muslim and a Serb can move anywhere in the country.

We're protecting the integrity of the IEBL (Inter-Entity Boundary Line), we're policing the police out here and the police are our biggest problem we've got right now – the Croatian police crossing the IEBL, going into the wrong side, and the Serb police doing exactly the same. On my first week up in the hills I had quite a few problems with Croat police and on three occasions we chased them off and sorted them out.

> we're policing the police out here and the police are our biggest problem we've got right now – the Croatian police crossing the IEBL, going into the wrong side, and the Serb police doing exactly the same.

The local police are perfectly aware of what they're allowed to do. The Croatian policeman has to stay on the Federation side, he's not allowed to cross the IEBL into the Serb area, and they're perfectly aware of that. They keep trying it on. By mounting patrols and actually waiting for them you can surprise them and when you do see them you basically tell them where to go and we'll turn them back – and they will do that. The other thing we're doing is mounting checkpoints, they're only allowed to mount checkpoints for thirty minutes and if they stay there for any longer we will go and move them on.

As long as peace holds and the more they try and build up industry here, and the busier the roads get, the tanks will start to get in the way a bit. Up in the hills though, it's quite a shock for them to see a tank rolling up. A lot of the police are ex-Army and when they see a main battle tank like this trundling around they just disappear the moment we turn up. They've got a lot of respect for that kind of weight travelling around the countryside, they really have."

Previous page.
Commander of Warrior Infantry Fighting Vehicle speeds through a small village near Mrkonic Grad. The Warriors are protected by the latest 'Chobham' type composite armour.

Opposite.
Challenger tank and crew stop for a rest in a rural part of western Bosnia, near Mrkonic Grad.

# Marlin Rowe

PRIVATE, DRIVER OF WARRIOR
WORCESTERSHIRE & SHERWOOD FORESTERS

### Interviewed in Stroica village

"Half of these drivers are out of their head and most of them are drunk while they're driving. The number of RTAs, that's Road Traffic Accidents, caused by the locals on slivovic, is incredible. They're all over the road. IFOR troops stick to the speed limit.

I've had a couple of very close shaves. There's a big forest over there and they've got these big lorries. As they come down the road some of the brake systems on them go. One was tramming down the hill – and we were coming up it – and it shot round the corner and I wanged my brakes on, we can stop to a dead halt within the length of the Warrior. He came tramming towards us and he had to pull out. If I hadn't have stopped he would have hit us, and he would have come off worse, he would have gone off the cliff – definitely.

I think the IFOR role should have been used at the start, we should be UN by now, then we could have got to grips with the fighting. It's all right, we came up here and this school was all covered in debris. We cleared it out and as soon as we started we had the locals, all the kids, everybody, come to help and I thought, 'At least they want to make a difference for themselves.' We used to play football with them at night and they used to invite us up for coffee and everything. We thought we had achieved something. These people up here are quite friendly, they'd do anything for you.

Bosnia's all right but it's like anywhere. The general population want to get their lives back together again, it's the minority who are quite happy to sit back and let IFOR build things up for them, and when it's done step back in there and take advantage.

I'm married and I've got kids back home, I'm from Chesterfield."

# George MacGinnes

MAJOR, 3RD ARMOURED ENGINEER SQUADRON

### Interviewed at bridge over Sana River

"The basic story we have here is we're on the Sana River, just south of Sanski Most, and as you look out you can see the old demolished bridge. This river line was held as a defensive position by the Serbs as the Federation forces swept north from Kljuc up towards Sanski Most. As the Serbs fell back they blew the bridge, leaving the obstacle.

In the aftermath, the Federation Forces put in a pontoon bridge immediately adjacent to that and you'll see that it's not maintained and it's vulnerable to the fast flowing water in the spring floods. So, what we had always intended to do was come down to this site and build a permanent bridge clear of the water, on good foundations, to re-open the route permanently to heavy traffic. In February, the Royal Engineers came down here to do that and they started excavating along the abutments of the original, now demolished, bridge and they uncovered a mass grave. That grave is believed to contain Muslim victims of the Serb atrocities of some years before, and this discovery then halted our work until the ICTY were able to come and carry out a proper exhumation and investigation into what was there.

Top left.
George MacGinnis, a major in the Royal Engineers, explaining the situation with the bridge near Sanski Most.

Top right.
Domnic Roberts, Commander of a platoon of Challenger tanks on patrol in a rural area to the south of Mrkonic Grad.

Bottom.
Marlin Rowe, driver of a Warrior Infantry Fighting Vehicle, in the village of Stroica.

That whole process took about three months and, in the meantime, they needed a temporary bypass which was good enough for much of the civilian traffic. But, as you can see with the wooden infill of the gap in the centre, it's actually relatively unsafe and difficult to traffic. So, what we're coming to do is a long term, permanent solution for heavy traffic capable of taking the most difficult civilian vehicles such as buses – which have trouble getting up and down steep ramps.

Where we stand now is an upgraded crossing we have created to free up the site that they're actually going to work on, and allow free civilian access. We're constructing the main abutments for a bridge and will put in something capable of taking up to a hundred tons of traffic. The whole process, from start to finish of our arrival on site, will be just over three weeks long."

# Joanne Mallin

## CAPTAIN, BRIGADE COMMANDER OF ROYAL MILITARY POLICE

### Interviewed at Brigade HQ, Sipovo

"I'm in charge of all the military policemen and women in this brigade. The primary role is to keep the routes clear and signed between Split and Banja Luka. If there are any traffic accidents we investigate, then clear the way. We control all traffic when units change. I've got sixty two people and twenty three vehicles. It's never enough but we manage.

We've been able to take on the role of social patrolling, or community policing, in and around the towns. It was decided to move all the heavy looking equipment and heavy armour out of Sipovo so I seized the opportunity to let my guys do the patrolling here. We've got soft approach vehicles, Land Rovers, and just pistols. We can get in among the people and have a chat with them and find out what their problems are, what their concerns are. Do they know about the elections? Have they got water?

There's a big problem over here about traffic accidents. Civilian drivers are a bit loony and they create traffic accidents. We've got drivers with big heavy vehicles, and when they've been driving all day they cause accidents. At the moment we're handing out a lot of leaflets about avoiding accidents.

Since the weather cleared up and all the snow melted, all the routes are now fairly clear. It's an opportunity (for IFOR people) to put the foot down and get to where you're going – and we found we had a speeding problem. We've got speed guns and we go out and do speed traps, when we pull somebody over we also check that they're carrying all the equipment they're supposed to have over here: helmet, body armour, rations, survival kit and all that kind of business.

We're trying to keep people aware that we're actually still on operations. A lot of vehicles have been here for a long time and we have a mechanic with us to check the tyres and everything. It really is a way of protecting the force, protecting our guys.

Traditionally, the Military Police are always the bad guys, the people who arrest you and throw you in jail and get you into trouble. But out here we actually live with these people, so if we go out and be pedantic about every little offence that we see, life with them is not going to be too pleasant. Actually, out here we have found that we don't need to do it anyway because everybody is so busy doing their job. It's an operational tour,

Top.
Old and new bridges near Sanski Most in western Bosnia. The civilian bridge was destroyed by retreating Serb forces and replaced by a Bosnian army pontoon bridge which in turn was replaced by an IFOR Bailey bridge. This is now being replaced by a permanent construction being built by British Army engineers.

Bottom.
Joan Mallin, a captain in the Royal Military Police, stands by her Landrover at British Brigade HQ, Sipovo.

we're all trained for it and we're doing a lot of training while we're out here, so actually policing these soldiers is pretty low on my list of priorities. A commanding officer will call me up to say, 'There's been an incident. Can you come and have a look at it for me?' We'll respond to a request rather than going looking for work. There isn't a crime rate within the military community here.

The IPTF (the International Police Task Force) is a UN organisation and its mission is to help, monitor, advise and train the civilian police here so they adopt internationally recognised measures of human rights and law enforcement. They're pretty multi-national and they're supposed to spend all their time with the civilian police, monitoring what they're doing, advising them on the best way to do things.

Freedom of movement is the big issue here and the civilian police like to do checkpoints everywhere. IPTF have to prevent that to make sure people have freedom of movement and if there is a crime or an accident to investigate it properly. Nothing will go forward if the freedom of movement issue isn't solved; they know that if they don't comply there will never be elections, nothing will ever happen. They've had their problems because they've been thrown together and they don't know each other very well.

The IPTF don't have anywhere to live, they don't have any resources of their own and their vehicles are pretty thin on the ground. But as time has gone by they've started to sort that out and they have money to support themselves now. They've latched onto the military because we're able to support them, but they don't understand the military so it's a slow process."

# Andy Cooney

## SERGEANT, 2/2 ENGINEER BATTALION

### Interviewed at Brigade HQ, Sipovo

"I'm responsible for collating and distributing information about known or suspected minefields, and I go out and brief IFOR troops and civilians on the threat of mines. Over the past four or five years, war has ravaged this country, and the tide of the war has ebbed and flowed backwards and forwards and, because of this movement, a great deal of minefields have been laid across the country, mostly along former confrontation lines. A lot of the minefields we have records for and these aren't such a problem. However, there are minefields that are unmarked and unknown and these ones are causing great problems to IFOR troops and civilians.

A great deal has changed in the country over the last couple of years: peoples' attitudes, peoples' ideals, the political situation. There is now a peace agreement, although this is very fragile, between the former warring factions. The only thing that hasn't changed is the threat from mines; they're still in the ground, some have been in the ground for five or six years, they're in an unstable state, they're not marked or identified and they're a real danger to civilians and IFOR troops.

It is my job to make sure troops and civilians are aware of these dangers and to try and advise and warn them on the actions they should carry out if they do encounter mines or unexploded ordnance.

There are five basic rules. First, you should never leave any tarmac or concrete roads

Top.
Royal Military Police on patrol with members of IPTF (International Police Task Force) in Sipovo. The IPTF have the responsibility of training and monitoring the local Bosnian police forces and they rely on IFOR for backup and support.

Bottom.
A strategic bridge on the main southern route into Banja Luka, the biggest town in the Republika Srpska entity within Bosnia. This bridge was destroyed by NATO aircraft in late 1995. Traffic is now diverted through a new road carved into the cliffside by British Royal Engineers.

Overleaf.
View of a Bosnian village near Prozor in central Bosnia.

because these have been cleared to a width of five metres by our engineering teams. Secondly, you should not drive on any verges. These are littered with mines. As people come back to their fields to tend their crops they find anti-personnel mines; they pick these up and place them on the side of the road, thinking that IFOR troops will come along and pick them up. What tends to happen is that IFOR troops come along and usually end up driving over them.

The third rule is, do not go souvenir hunting. It's a great British tradition that everyone likes to go home with a momento of where they've been and what they've done. The tendency is to start wandering around fields or old confrontation lines looking for bits of old ordnance like helmets or bayonets or empty shell cases. By doing this you run the risk of treading on or tripping over a mine.

Also we say do not enter any uncleared buildings. As the war was fought through the country people were obviously driven from their houses and, as a last defiant gesture, they would throw down anti-personnel mines around the property – if you enter you run the risk of killing or injuring yourself.

> From an early age children
> were taught the principles of
> mine warfare in schools.
> They are very, very knowledgeable
> about the subject.

The majority of IFOR troops are very mine conscious, in fact you have to congratulate a great deal of them because part of my job is to collate all the sightings of mines and unexploded ordnance that IFOR troops encounter. A lot of them are very alert and see these items lying around and they follow the correct procedure which is to mark them and report them.

However, there's always the lunatic fringe that wants to flaunt the rules, I don't know whether it's through boredom, or adventure or plain naiveté but there are troops on the ground who are not sticking to these rules and they are moving around in undeclared areas. These troops are of concern to me. So far we've been lucky we haven't had a major incident.

There was an incident on 28th January when an armoured vehicle drove over an anti-tank mine, resulting in the loss of three British soldiers. A very tragic event that really brought home the problem of mines in Bosnia. They were on a route that was known to be clear but, it turned out, it wasn't clear. This is a problem we're having; no route is clear unless it's been cleared by an engineer disposal team.

The mine in question was the TMR-P6 anti-tank mine. It contains about five kilograms of explosive but also has a Miznay-Schardin steel plate. As the mine explodes this plate forms what we call a 'shape' charge, and this is projected upwards at a speed of six thousand metres per second and it will penetrate about four hundred millimetres of armour. As it explodes the plate forms a hot molten slug, rather like a pointed missile, which is projected forward at such a speed that it punches right through the thickest armour. The belly side of a tank is very vulnerable to mines and the TMR-P6 is highly effective against most of the vehicles we have in Theatre. Every week we get sighting reports of the TMR-P6 mines, although the state of the undergrowth is making spotting them increasingly difficult.

The Bosnians took their mine warfare very seriously. From an early age children were taught the principles of mine warfare in schools. They are very, very knowledgeable about the subject. A lot of the mines they've got are highly effective. There is an anti-personnel mine called the PROM-1 and when that detonates it will leap 0.7 metres into the air and explode, it's lethal to a range of about fifty metres. A lot of the anti-tank mines are non-metallic so tracing them with metal detectors is virtually impossible."

## THE BRITISH GUNS

# Matt Dahlberg

BOMBARDIER, ROYAL ARTILLERY, AS90 TEAM

### Interviewed at Gun Battery near Mrkonic Grad

"The AS90 has hydro gas suspension so it's a very comfortable ride. It can carry a crew of five inside and weighs forty six tons. It is designed to be a forward fighting machine with a range of twenty four thousand, seven hundred metres, so we can operate quite a way back from the battle area. This gun is 'Fire and Movement', somebody can call for fire and we can hit a position in about a minute and a half, we can bring round a three round burst in ten seconds – and then we can be on the move again. We have our own navigational system on board.

We can hit infantry dug-in, armoured vehicles, soft skinned vehicles, anything. The type of tank we come across here, the T-72 and T-55, we could take out with one of these, purely through the strike force of the shell. Anything in the capability of the Challenger or the M1 – not a chance. If you hit one of those tanks you would seriously damage the crew inside through the shock and impact, however the tank wouldn't be too devastated.

The only rounds we have with us at the moment are smoke illuminating marker rounds, practise flash rounds and high explosive rounds. On the high explosive rounds we have a multi-role fuse on it so we can actually set the round to go off at various height settings, or we can have a delayed setting so it can go off 0.025 metres into the ground – that's for dug-in infantry. The forward observers will tell us exactly what we're firing at and the set orders that we get will include ammunition orders, exactly what we've got to get in there.

> The flash rounds are especially for use in Bosnia. When it detonates all that will happen is there will be a big flash of smoke and a little flash. It's basically a warning to whoever it may be, Serbs, Croats or whoever, that we can put down a round, wherever, very accurately.

The flash rounds are especially for use in Bosnia. When it detonates all that will happen is there will be a big flash of smoke and a little flash. It's basically a warning to whoever it may be, Serbs, Croats or whoever, that we can put down a round, wherever, very accurately. It could be used to break up warring factions, if they were massed on the road you could bring it down by the side of them, perhaps a hundred metres away in a field.

These guns are the most accurate artillery pieces in service in any army in the world at the moment. I love working on them because I've worked on guns before that are very much lifting heavy weights, really hard graft, whereas the work on this is more technical. The rounds themselves are the hard work, the lifting, that's why there's so many men – a ten man crew. It's a hundred pound shell and lifting that around soon tires you out. When the UN were here the Warriors stuck out as the thing that impressed the warring factions, but now it's the AS90s and the Challengers. If it was me I wouldn't like to mess around with the Challenger or the AS90, they really are powerful bits of kit. Overall it has made

a big impression. The locals seem very pleased to see us in the civilian areas.

I've been twelve years in man-service, and of those twelve years about ten of those have been in guns, different guns. You can have the trades, which say this man can do the job, however experience is what you need really. A battery of six guns has the support of 150 guys. Retention in the army is pretty bad, that's basically the problem we have. You get gunners who you're just starting to train up and they're just looking at getting their first step to promotion – that's when they normally make the decision to stay in or get out. If they get out, that's all that time and money wasted. The other night we were trying to work out why retention and recruitment are such a problem, and we couldn't put it down to any one thing, it's hard to put your thumb exactly on it. Times have changed big-style in the Army; in some ways for the good, in some ways for the bad, but it's really hard to say, 'This was better, this was worse'.

My mates back in Nottingham all thought I was off my head when I joined. I've seen a few of them since and some of them have said, 'Maybe I should have given it a go'. People think, 'Oh no, it's the Army, it's going to be shouting and bawling'. But it's not like that. The telly does give a certain perspective of the Army, that Windsor Davies type perspective.

When we sit around in here, in the gun, it's not 'Sergeant Cook, Bombardier Dahlberg', it's Nick, Matt and so on, we work as a little team. If an officer walks up then it's 'Sergeant Cook', we play the game, but it's like one little family here. We've got a very, very good crew on this gun. That's one thing that's changed for the better in the Army. When I first joined the regiment you didn't speak to anybody unless you were spoken to, that was the way it was. The thing I remember most about joining the Army was thinking, 'You're on your own'. But here we've got a new lad in and we're thinking, 'Let's get him in, let's speak to him, let's find out what he likes'. He's only been with us for a couple of weeks and we've tried to bring him in, to get to know him. You've got to make him feel like part of the family. There's nothing worse than a young lad coming out here and nobody talks to him. He's in a strange place, strange environment, strange people, you've got to make him feel welcome.

There are thousands of people in the Army and they are all individuals. Perhaps they've had a bad time but you get that in all walks of life. You make your own bed in the Army; if you walk around with attitude and you give people attitude you're going to get nowhere. If you start putting effort into the things that you do, you get noticed; when you start getting noticed you start going up the ranks, you start doing trades and you start getting paid for it. It is decent money. You work hard and you can play hard – although a lot of it seems just work hard at the moment.

If I had left when I was a gunner, I dread to think what I would be doing now. I'd probably have gone to work down the pit and that would have closed. I dread to think. In all walks of life you have your ups and downs, I've had a few ups and downs in the Army, and I thought, 'Maybe I should have made a break then, maybe I shouldn't'. But what is there to get out to? What is there out there?

I see my mates at home and, all right, some of them did well, they took their chances, but the ones that are doing well are the ones in the stable job all the way through, with a career-type structure in it. The rest of them are either on the dole or they're flitting between jobs every few months. I couldn't deal with that, especially now that I'm married, with a little girl. This is it. I've made the Army my career and that's going to be it now, I've made my decision, I'm going to go for it."

Top.
Sergeant Nick Cook (on right)
and Bombardier Matt Dahlberg
(on left) sit on top of the
AS90 self propelled gun.
Sergeant Cook is the 'number one'
on this gun and only he can
give the order to fire. Bombardier
Dahlberg is the 'number two'.

Bottom.
AS90 self propelled gun coming
out of its 'garage' with only three
inches to spare on either side.

95

# Danny Wileman

GUNNER, ROYAL ARTILLERY, AS90 TEAM

**Interviewed at Gun Battery near Sipovo**

"I don't know why I joined the Army, there was no family history behind it. I was just walking along the street one day and I passed the Army Careers Office and I decided to pop in. They made it sound really good, they really dramatised it, but in reality . . .

Did a year's basic training, as a sixteen year old, then joined the regular army. We got deployed to Bosnia as the first stage of IFOR troops, us and the Americans, on January 12th. It was horrendous, hell on earth. The first place was an old slaughterhouse at Mrkonic Grad. When we got there we found dead animals everywhere, it stank, freezing cold, raining, mud up to your knees, full of crap in the hangers. It was abysmal, beyond human living anyway.

We laid down pallets of wood and slept on top of them for the first few nights and then we cleared out the hangar. It was full of flour and mice and everything you could name and then, with old chicken coops, we made some basic shelving so we could sleep somewhere for a few weeks. Eventually we got some tents and we took all the shelving down and lived in the tents. As the weather improved the conditions started to get better.

I worked on the guns for about a year and a half before coming out here. Without camouflage netting it's okay, but with the cam net it's really hard work. Really, it's boring more than anything else. Just sitting around all day, just showing your presence. The actual gun is all right once you're firing because there's quite a lot to do loading the shells, but we've been doing dry, static deployments, just sitting there. We went firing down at Glamoc firing range, about twelve rounds in three days, so there's not much happening there.

This is the worst country I've been to, it's horrible. It's the aftermath of the war, especially in a poor area like this. Mrkonic Grad has been hit really hard. You feel sorry for the people, going back to their houses, devastated, nothing to go back to, little children running around in rags. You're just glad you're not living here yourself, just glad that you're going home soon. I'm glad to be getting out of here personally – good luck to the next one coming out."

# Jonathon Tomlinson

GUNNER, 26 REGIMENT, ROYAL ARTILLERY, AS90 TEAM

**Interviewed at Gun Battery near Sipovo**

"I've always wanted to be in the Army. The first couple of years I liked it but then it started to fade away. I don't like doing these six month tours, it's too far away. They should only do two or three months max, it would give you more chance to go to more places.

It's really an awful place, terrible – ruins everywhere. There was nobody about for the first couple of months, saw no one. After about the middle of April everyone started coming back and then it started to go a bit faster and we started to see people. I think IFOR is going well."

Top left.
Billy Gage, a gunner with a Royal Artillery AS90 team, about to go on guard duty at the gun battery near Sipovo.

Top right.
Jay Armstrong, the driver of an AS90 self propelled gun, sits in the grass at the gun battery near Sipovo.

Bottom.
The AS90 self propelled gun can fire three 155mm shells within ten seconds, at distances up to 24 kilometres, at the gun battery near Sipovo.

IFOR
on
IFOR

# Jay Armstrong

DRIVER, 26 REGIMENT, ROYAL ARTILLERY, AS90 DRIVER

**Interviewed at Gun Battery near Sipovo**

"You do get a lot of stares when you're driving, but it handles okay apart from snowy conditions, when it can get a little out of hand sometimes and skids and slides around a bit. It's a good fun vehicle to drive even though you may look at it and think, 'Big monster, scary thing to drive'. So far I haven't hit any drivers, even though I've had some close shaves.

I do believe that over here they don't take a driving test of any description, they're just driving a car somewhere. You'll come face to face with them on the hairpins and the first thing they see is our big bow and they tend to drive towards you because they're staring at the vehicle rather than paying attention to the road. Because we all know each other rather well now, you do in a six month tour, it's all based on Mickey taking. I've got ginger hair and so I get such nice nicknames as 'Ginge' and 'Firehead'. It's sort of fun, Mickey taking, you can't afford to have a bad sense of humour, you've got to laugh it off at the end of the day.

I joined the Army because at the time I was a little bit bored. I was at college and I happened to be passing an Army Careers Office and I thought, 'Hey, I've seen all those glorified advertisements, I'll pop my head in and have a look'. They showed me a few videos and I thought, 'This looks good' – vehicles whizzing across country, helicopters flying around. So I thought 'yeah' and sat the exam.

The bloke behind the counter talked me into joining the artillery because he was an artillery person – not a very good decision, I could have done better, could have done engineering of some description. On the actual tests they can grade you on what you can actually do and I was offered nearly everything but because the bloke behind the desk was artillery he persuaded me to join.

I was the only one of my group of friends to join the Army. In a way they found it quite amusing, they said, 'What are you on Jay? You're joining the Army man, going away for long periods of time'. Now they're saying, 'You've done long enough, it's about time you called it a day and chilled out a little bit more.' I've done just over six years.

I came here a day before these guys. I had to pick up the vehicle off the ferry, so I spent a day down in Split where I thought, 'Hey, this ain't bad, this is something else, I can relate to this'. As I came into Bosnia it hit us. It was devastated, they were still burning houses at the time, the roads were not very passable, big craters in the road, pretty hectic. There were no people, they had just got up and left everything, left their possessions, their cars. In some areas we were driving through you could see they'd left their cars in the garages and just gone.

It was a lonely place: lonely, cold, unwanted, unloved countryside. Split was a warm place. I was welcomed off the aeroplane, not bad people, all waves and smiles, having a look round for the girls – and there did seem to be a lot of them. Up here you didn't see many people at all."

> As I came into Bosnia it hit us. It was devastated, they were still burning houses at the time, the roads were not very passable, big craters in the road, pretty hectic. There were no people, they had just got up and left everything, left their possessions, their cars.

Top.
A Chinook transport helicopter delivers a 105mm light artillery piece to soldiers of the Royal Artillery who shelter from the Chinook's downdraught by a Landrover. These guns can be assembled and firing in less than four minutes.

Bottom.
A British artilleryman looks out of the back of a Chinook transport helicopter as it comes in to land at Glamoc live firing range.

# Billy Gage

GUNNER, ROYAL ARTILLERY, AS90 TEAM

### Interviewed at Gun Battery near Sipovo

"I was having a bit of a 'mare on civvy street and I thought this would be a good way out, to sort my life out, otherwise I would have ended up in the nick. I was doing various nocturnal activities and I got caught a few times, I was with the wrong crowd. This has helped, I've sorted myself out, I've got myself a nice Mrs. I've been in about two years now.

Not really many people want to join the Army in this day and age, everyone's too into the partying and the E-scene and everything else. I've often thought about getting out but then you think to yourself, 'What am I going to do if I get out?' You build yourself up on this level and you think you're better than everybody else, better than the whole civilian population, and you think, 'Oh my God, I'm going to be like one of them, one of them numbers', and you're caught between two worlds.

To tell you the truth I just want to be out of this regiment, it's not for me. It's too static, boring, full of bullshit. Down by the vehicles, there are some stones; they'll have you placing the stones up against the side and painting the steps. You're on an operational tour and it's so annoying it's unbelievable.

> **I'm putting my life at risk for something I don't really believe in, and all I'm getting all day is shit.**

As a gunner I do loading, laying, sorting out ammunition, various things. It's good when you're on the gun, but when you're back in camp time goes so slow it's unbelievable. We're out on the gun maybe three days out of every week and a half, then you come back and it's nightmare again. Daily routine here: go on troop parade about 9 o'clock when they call your name to make sure you're still here. They check your ammo and morphine and documentation. Once that's checked you normally go to the Q Store and sign out some brushes and then you start sweeping the day away and that's all you do.

They allow you to go running out of the camp, but they won't allow you to go into town to associate with the people. Two beer can rule. They should sort out some adventure training areas. It's really getting everyone down here, everyone's on a total minus because they're bored and because of all the bullshit, because of all the senior ranks giving this day in, day out; daft little things that don't need to be done.

I'm on a six month tour here, I'm putting my life at risk for something I don't really believe in, and all I'm getting all day is shit. I could just do with a little time to myself to sort myself out – and it's just not happening. I think it's just this regiment but, saying that, every regiment you go to is just the same old shit.

The place itself? I think they've Mullah'd it completely, it's a right shithole. I don't think this could happen at home. Put it this way: I think we're too civilised and uncivilised at the same time to let something like this happen. We've got a mixture of both worlds in England, haven't we? We've got uncivilised people, civilised people and they both mix together in some strange way – but out here they don't mix at all.

There's a definite class system in the Army. If you've been to Eton or somewhere – you're an officer – and if you've just come off the street, you may be more intelligible than them, but you're just another number because you didn't go to public school, you didn't go and do further education.

It gets really nightmarish, it gets you really wound up because you get officers coming

A Scimitar light reconnaissance vehicle passes two Serbian women on the road to Mrkonic Grad. These fast vehicles provide the AS90 and other gun crews with target information that enables 'indirect fire' to take place. In other words they can shoot at a grid reference rather than a target that is visible to the eye.

onto your gun, and they haven't got a clue how to do anything on it, not a thing, they wouldn't even know how to load it, half of them, and they're giving it 'Do this, do that'. I reckon there should still be a rank structure but I think you should all be equal. They say it's based on merit but what it's based on is who can get the brownest tongue at the end of the day."

# Paul Milwood

GUNNER, 26 REGIMENT, ROYAL ARTILLERY, AS90 TEAM

### Interviewed at Gun Battery near Sipovo

"The class system; they won't associate with us, it's sickening sometimes. It's not that I want to go out on the piss with them or anything, but if you say something to them they look down their noses at you as if you're nothing, especially if you're a gunner. If you talk to a captain or anything, he's like 'all right, go away.' He's not interested at all. If you've got an idea, and everyone else thinks it's a good idea, and you tell him it's, 'Oh no, my idea is better'. You've just got no say in the matter. It's stupid.

If you do something right, or something good, it's never recognised. From Sergeant down, from Staff Sergeant down – yeah – but Warrant Officer up – that's it. You don't get recognised at all. But the sergeants do put a good word in for you, or try to, but they don't really have a lot of influence. If I was due for promotion the sergeants don't sit on the Promotion Board, it's just Warrant Officer upwards, but all they can say is what they've heard from a sergeant.

I think it's getting worse. I've been in the Army for five years now and it's just people with tongues down the back of people's trousers, that's it. If a staff sergeant wants to get promoted to Warrant Officer, he will just go for it – sod the lads, sod everything else."

# Mark Andrews

PRIVATE, WORCESTERSHIRE AND SHERWOOD FORESTERS

### Interviewed at Jezero village, near Mrkonic Grad

"It's a lot more low key than in Northern Ireland, you have to be a bit more friendly, learning how to speak to people, to deal with their everyday needs, to look after people. Being in infantry is definitely the best job in the Army. We're the brunt of everything, the front end, we do all what I think is basically the good work. It's a lot better than being sat in a Land Rover all day, driving from here to Split, you get to actually meet the people on the ground.

The patrol formation we use is always staggered, that's how we're trained. If we come under fire we simply get down, lay fire down and extract out of the danger area, keep going all the way until we're out of contact. At the same time I'd be sending back reports on my radio. We would then set up an incident control point and all the different agencies would look at where the fire came from.

You don't get taught to shoot in the legs, you wouldn't fire on somebody if you didn't want him dead. We get taught to shoot to kill and use as minimum rounds as possible, so if you shoot him, and he goes down, you wouldn't just keep shooting him, we don't class that as professional. You shoot him once, that's it. We're taught one shot, one kill; aim for the centre body all the time.

> You don't get taught to shoot in the legs, you wouldn't fire on somebody if you didn't want him dead.

Our gun is heavier than most. Special Forces wouldn't choose this weapon because it's too heavy. It's 5.56 and it has a lot of stoppages on the ranges. It's all right though, it does the job. The M-16 is a much lighter weapon and the AK47 is more reliable, they're widely used and the preferred weapon of most people.

I don't see the point of us being here, it's not our war."

# Lawrence Crabb

LIEUTENANT, WORCESTERSHIRE & SHERWOOD FORESTORS

### Interviewed at Omici village, near Jezero

"Our platoon can go on training missions which is absolutely brilliant because we're living in villages, going on patrols, maintaining an IFOR presence and securing base camps. Every three or four weeks we can drop everything and go back to the role of an Infantry Battalion, and get into the field. Infantry need to be able to close in and kill the enemy so we go up to the Dubrina ranges and assume the role of dismounted infantry so we can hone those skills: patrolling skills, section attacks, fighting skills, map reading,

watermanship training – if we encounter a huge lake we strip down to the undies, make a flotation pack and swim to the other side and continue.

We're based at Jezero which is located at the bottom of the Anvil. It's a very strategic location at the centre of several important roads that converge in this massively hilly area. We're now at the village of Omici which is a small village of Muslim people, an enclave of about thirty five people at the top of a hill. During the war these people stayed here, being helped by the Serbs at the bottom of the hill.

When the HVO rolled through the Serbs split and did a runner up north and the Muslims again stayed here. They were left alone. When the Serbs came back and re-occupied their houses at the bottom they found that a lot of their kit was missing, and their houses were ruined – much the same as everywhere else in the country. The Serbs then came to the top of the hill and identified a few cattle and chickens and they accused the Muslims of stealing them – and that's basically the problem we have here. The Liaison Officers and the police have been involved and there are now even Court Orders on cows belonging to the people who say they are theirs.

It's something we can't really get involved in, it's a very slow process. If the Muslims have stolen the cows they're very well hidden, it's not at all obvious, but obviously somebody is going to know what their cow looks like and we are not. We can't have a judging view on whose cow it is, because that would mean we were siding with a certain faction.

The Serbs irregularly have a few drinks, come up the top of the hill and, without the help of the law, are trying to solve it themselves. They try and say, 'Look, this is my cow. If you don't give it back we're going to beat you up.' We are here to stop any trouble happening and if we were to pull out there would be big trouble up here.

We did quite an extensive survey up here and found that they haven't really got a problem with the locals here, the Serbs at the bottom of the hill. It's the Serbs from other areas, like Sipovo, that are the problem. Having talked to everybody in different areas I can see it's not that bad, it's really calmed down. There's no underlying hatred between the units, it's just bits left over from the war.

I've seen movements of displaced people coming to visit their homes, which are now being occupied by other people – it's all open arms. It's happening all over our area of operations. From what I've seen, in the future they will be living together. We've only scratched the surface but there is a lot of friendship still. I've talked to people in Stroica and they were best of friends before the war. You've got split marriages, Serb, Croat, Muslim and they were saying, 'Why should we fight now? We were the best of friends before the war.' They really are against all this fighting and hatred, all they want to do is get on with their lives. There's a lot of unease still and they can only meet in certain places, where they feel safe from police harassment, but the general feeling is that they want to get on with it and get back to normal.

They are so friendly it's unbelievable. They will do anything, literally anything for you. They only get so much aid, a couple of kilos of flour for a month, they've got no money, no jobs and most of them are refugees – yet they would give you their last piece of bread, their last dime, to see you happy."

A British Infantry soldier waits for orders and leans against the Warrior Infantry Vehicle.

# Hari Bahadurgurung

## CORPORAL, ROYAL GHURKHA RIFLES

**Interviewed at Brigade HQ, Sipovo**

"My service in the British Army is running on twelve years now and I have a lot of experience. My regiment is part of the 5th Airborne Brigade in the UK. I have been to Hong Kong, Brunei, Hawai, Malaysia, United Kingdom and Nepal itself.

When we first came here everyone was excited. We had a bit of a hard time at first, we had a lot of jobs to do: guarding the multi-national Division North Headquarters, doing VIP escorts, building the defence positions, et cetera.

After a couple of months it went all right and we had a chance to learn the Serbo-Croat language. Some of my boys are very good in Serbo-Croat, they can speak fluently. The general public here like Ghurkas, when we go round the town they can speak with us. Most of my boys can speak the language. According to me it will go all right over here. The general people will understand the problem and I think they will all again live together in a peaceful way.

In the last two world wars we fought against the Japanese, alongside British soldiers. We live in hill towns in Nepal and we are very active in hand to hand fighting. In World War One and Two they did not have very good weapons, like they do now, they had to fight with swords and we were good at that.

Our forefathers defeated the Japanese and people all over the world came to know that the Ghurkas were good at fighting. The British Government found us very loyal and faithful and that is why we are still serving with them."

# Vsuwan Singh Rai

## PRIVATE, ROYAL GHURKA RIFLES

**Interviewed at Brigade HQ, Sipovo**

"I joined six years ago and am enjoying my responsibilities very much. I will be a private during all my service because it is entirely depending on vacancies for promotion. I am doing a driver's job in Bosnia and also improving my Serbo-Croat language so I can speak with the civilians. I can understand what they say and I can understand what they want.

I've been to four or five places in Bosnia during my tour. It's been nearly seven months now and most of the people do not want to help each other. If I'm speaking to a Muslim, the Croat doesn't like me speaking to someone else. I think they have to change their minds, they have to live together. I told them a Muslim, a Croat, a Serb are the same thing for me. They ask me if I like Muslims and I say, 'Yes, I do', and they say, 'How about us? And I say, 'Yes, I like everybody, everybody is the same for me' and they say, 'it's okay'.

The children are looking for good relations and we can talk their language and this makes them very happy. If we can't answer them in their language they will be really unhappy, they will think, 'Oh, why didn't you want to speak with us?' Most of the IFOR personnel can't speak their language.

The Ghurkas can survive in tropical countries, Arctic countries, wherever. We can learn many languages as well. For example, serving in Hong Kong we can speak a bit of the

Top left.
Vsuwan Singh Rai on guard duty at the gate of British Brigade HQ at Sipovo.

Top right.
Hari Bahadurgurung of the 3rd Royal Ghurkas, off duty at the Brigade HQ, Sipovo.

Bottom.
Bosnian Serb villagers, mainly elderly, queue up at British IFOR landrover for weekly food ration distribution, Stroica village.

Chinese language, living in Brunei we can speak Malaysian, we can speak the Indian languages, plus our own language. We can speak seven or eight languages so we are very interested in building up new languages as well.

We have a small guide-book for basic words, many of these words sound like our language but, basically, we are not allowed to go outside without a weapon. Those chidren who come up to the gate give us a very good opportunity to practise the language. Most of the Bosnian pronunciation and letters are very similar to the Ghurka language, so we find it very easy. British guys would find it very difficult and also they would not have sufficient time to learn the language."

# Mike Leudicke

## LIEUTENANT, QUEEN'S LANCASHIRE REGIMENT

### Interviewed at 'Precision Factory' base, Gornji Vakuf

"We do a lot of surveys in villages around here and a lot of them see us simply as a peace-keeping force, and now there is a peace they see that our job is at an end. Because we're now breaking into other activities, for example trying to educate and inform people about the elections, people don't yet see that we're getting involved in those things and are sometimes hostile. We go around asking about their water supply, their electricity – because we can help in these areas – and people think we are being nosey and there's some ulterior motive to it. But we can help out.

Most of the communities are very small villages, and they are villages as they were in England a good few years ago; cut off communities where the most important man is the head man of the village, and not really anybody higher up the political chain. The main hierarchy in the towns and villages are probably viewed with the same respect as we would give to our national ministers.

They're cut off, the lives of these communities aren't developed at the moment, they have been damaged a lot. In a lot of the small towns and villages the only information they get is by word of mouth or things such as *The Herald of Peace*, the IFOR newspaper. When we first started dishing them out people said 'No, I don't want it' because they thought they would have to pay. But once they get a taster for it and realise that it is free, and that they like it they take as much as we can deliver.

The whole thing is developing now; because peace is here, and it seems to be lasting, we're able to deploy in any role our commanders see fit. We're really involved in G5 operations, the 'hearts and minds' side of things, using the skilled people we've got to get plastic in windows, repair walls, get rid of dead animals, re-paint walls, help out with the plumbing and sewage. All this is radically different to the training we had prior to coming out here, but it's something the guys are adapting to very well. It's very different to what the guys were expecting but the majority will go back having had a good experience, because it is doing good.

A lot of people who write to the guys still think it is a giant meat grinder out here. They think we're living day to day and there's still bad things going on. People have to realise it's all over now and the majority of people here, ninety nine per cent, are just interested in getting on with their lives in their village. It's not a hellhole anymore, it's just a basic society and they're trying to get on top and we're trying to help them do it."

Top.
A soldier of the Queen's Lancashire Regiment distributes election information in the town of Bugjonjo.

Bottom.
A British corporal in the Queen's Lancashire Regiment passes anti IFOR graffiti on an abandoned Croat house in the Muslim town of Bugjonjo.

# Nancy Mavis

## MAJOR, 16TH ARMOURED FIELD AMBULANCE

**Interviewed in Lubovo village, near Sipovo**

"We're in medical support to the IFOR troops but luckily there aren't any casualties at the moment, so therefore we're taking on more humanitarian tasks. Basically, a lot of these villages had small cottage hospitals, or Ambulantas, and what happened is that most of them were ransacked, destroyed and the drugs made totally useless. So, what we're doing is filling the gap until we can get the buildings weather-proofed, they get their doctors back into the area, then we hand over the connection we have with Medecins Sans Frontieres and they can run their own clinics again.

> Basically, a lot of these villages had small cottage hospitals, or Ambulantas, and what happened is that most of them were ransacked, destroyed and the drugs made totally useless.

We see a lot of patients, low grade chronic medical problems: arthritis, heart problems like angina, many diseases of the elderly, quite a lot of dental extractions, things that have been neglected during the period of conflict that people are now wanting to get treated again.

In the Anvil area the health service has very much been destroyed. It's in the process of being rebuilt. There's been a lot of funding requests from various areas and each town or community is looked at on its merits to see exactly what that hospital needs to restore it to what it was. This is done through the Liaison Officers in each area.

The local community appears to be very, very poor. The government here doesn't seem to have a lot of money either, although they are putting in the manpower to tidy things up. Everybody seems to be doing what they can."

Top.
Soldiers of the Queen's Lancashire Regiment make friends with children in the hardline Muslim town of Bugjonjo. Between the two British soldiers sits a Serbian translator.

Bottom.
Dr Nancy Mavis, a major in the British Army, treats a Serb villager for tooth trouble in a makeshift clinic in the small village of Lubovo, near Sipovo.

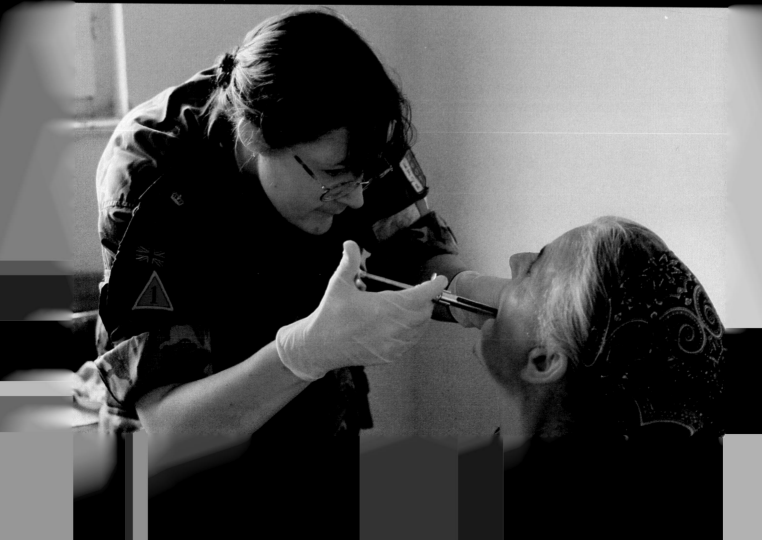

# THE MALAYSIAN BATTLE GROUP

## Bero Salim

SERGEANT MAJOR, MALAYSIAN BATTLE GROUP

### Interviewed at Malaysian HQ, Livno

"The administration is running very fine and so far there have been no disciplinary cases. There have been no threats from the locals surrounding the camp, in fact they're very friendly people.

Coming to Bosnia is one of the golden opportunities a soldier has because of the different climate, different environment, different people; you don't get these opportunities back in Malaysia.

Malaysia started serving abroad very early. In the 1960s we served in the Congo to begin with, then Namibia, Cambodia and Somalia under the UN flag and now we are serving in Bosnia under the NATO forces. We should feel proud for being about the only South East Asian country selected to serve under the NATO forces.

The soldiers who are actually in Theatre are selected soldiers, you would not just pick any soldiers, any Tom, Dick or Harry and just send him out here. They undergo a very stringent test before coming here and they should be proud of it. After comparisons with other soldiers in the Theatre I think we are on a par, if not of a quality higher than them because we have a very strict discipline."

## Amarjit Sidhu

MAJOR, MALAYSIAN BATTLE GROUP

### Interviewed at Livno Camp

"My great grandfather was brought in, as a policeman, by the British to what was then Malaya. They recruited a lot of Indians, Sikhs for that matter, from northern India and took them as policemen to Malaya. From then on, the family settled down, they did not go back to India. My grandfather was in the Police Force, and so were my grand-uncles, then came my dad; he was in the British prisons as a warder, and now it's me – in the Malaysian Army.

I joined in 1979 and was commissioned in 1981. I've seen a lot of things in service over the last seventeen years, I should say. In the early days we were fighting the CTs, that is the Communist Terrorists, up at the Border and life was tough. We had to be in the operational areas for two months, back to the base for pre-training and leave, then back in again for two months.

We used to be deployed at forward bases and go out on fighting patrols and reconnaissance patrols, to gather information about the movements of the CTs in the jungles. With this intelligence we would lay some ambushes or cordon off certain areas to get these people. The forests were very closed, dark areas and it is a high risk operation;

The Malaysian bugler tradition comes from the British colonial influence when wars were fought on horseback. The bugle was the best way of passing information to the soldiers so they could be ordered to advance, retreat or just come to the cook house door.

you have to be very alert and you've got to know your staff very well, also you've got to read and understand the movement of the CTs because more often than not they are people just like us, but there's probably something they leave behind, a mark for their comrades to move in, and we would go round on patrol identifying these marks.

You might see a 'V' mark on the bark of a tree, it might show the direction in which the group is moving, it may show a rendezvous point for that army two kilometres away from that junction. It carries a lot of meanings, so when you get all the various information and you put it together and you make its process 'intelligence', you are very close to catching these people.

I do not think we have an insurgency problem any more in Malaysia, it is over since 1992. We're now concentrating more on training for a conventional setting. However, we have a lot of these jungle bashing experiences, I should say, and we have had real counter insurgency warfare experience. We are now here in this country and looking at what we learned back home regarding conventional warfare. We can always fight a conventional war with our training and experience.

The British were once the masters in Malaysia, they ruled Malaysia for some time before independence on the 31st August 1957. Now, traditions die hard and they do not just fade away. Traditions carry a lot of meaning and basically the first Malaysian troops were moulded by the British; that was the Royal Malay Regiment and it was company strength. It has developed into a very big force today – the Malaysian Army. Those traditions still do exist; the parades, training, mess life are all essentially British. Of course the language of command has changed.

I think the Malaysians have performed very well under the UN flag, going back to the days we served in the Congo, Namibia, then Somalia and now Bosnia. If that amount of trust has been put into the Malaysian troops, we have to have some essence that is recognised at the international level. The other thing is that we are a multi-ethnic country, although religiously it's an Islam based country. A lot of people speak English, there's a lot of freedom of movement, you're free as a minority. I think the world recognises that and the economy continues to grow.

We have a very vocal Prime Minister and I take my hat off to him, he is a man to be recognised. He has supported the struggle of the Bosnian people, they were actually squeezed between two other groups – the Serbs and the Croats. Throughout history they were without any assistance or help and, while the whole world sympathised, there had to be some assistance for the Bosnians.

We are coming into a multi-ethnic country with a multi-ethnic background of our own and I think this helps us understand the people here. We are not here to serve any one religion or any one ethnic group, we are here to serve everyone. So, we are very impartial on that and we understand the human sentiments of the different religions.

In the Malaysian Army you've got the Muslims, the Chinese, the Christians, the Hindus and the Sikhs like me. I think it's very easy to work together. Here in Bosnia it will take some time before the hatred actually fades away among the ethnic groups.

> I think the Malaysians have performed very well under the UN flag, going back to the days we served in the Congo, Namibia, then Somalia and now Bosnia. If that amount of trust has been put into the Malaysian troops, we have to have some essence that is recognised at the international level.

Top.
Major Amarjit Sidhu, the Media Relations Officer for the Malaysian Battle Group, at the Malaysian Battle Group HQ, near Livno.

Bottom.
Children of IFOR local employees in the camp laundry at Camp Livno.

# Abdullah Abubakar

MAJOR, RELIGIOUS OFFICER, MALAYSIAN BATTLE GROUP

**Interviewed at Camp Livno**

"I am a specialist in Islamic studies as well as an Army officer. Islam is a very good discipline for the Army. Religion is very important because it teaches them self-discipline, loyalty to the leader, hard work. Everybody must pray only five times a day, but we don't force them to pray, only if they're free and they want to come. About seventy per cent come and pray. About ten Bosnian workers come to me every night to learn about prayer techniques.

There is something wrong with somebody who does not understand Islam and comes to a bad conclusion about it. The western world always makes a bad conclusion about Islam because they haven't studied Islamic guidance, the proper method, they have maybe heard some wrong information. I hope all the human beings understand before making a biased conclusion about Islam. It must be studied, it can be a good guide for anyone. Any conclusions should be based upon research, not on what some people are told, and then re-told that Islam is bad, Islam is very fierce, Islam is rude. Then there is something wrong. If anybody knows and studies the truth, we can meet on the basis of good virtue.

We need to teach all the people loyalty, to do their best in their jobs, to have responsibility to yourself, because one day you have responsibility for your whole life. The method of Islam is religion as a way of life; we have responsibilities to our families, our wives, our children, our community, our nation, upholding humanity and country."

> Islam is a very good discipline for the Army. Religion is very important because it teaches them self discipline, loyalty to the leader, hard work.

Top left.
Shoes outside the Malaysian Mosque at Camp Livno. Although Malaysia is a multi-ethnic country, the majority of its citizens are Muslim.

## THE DUTCH AND THE CANADIANS

## The Dutch Mortars

## Anonymous Dutch Soldier

### Interviewed at Mrkonic Grad

"To fit into the UK artillery chain of command we organised the unit into a battery: six mortars, 120 millimetre mortars. They have an effective range of one thousand one hundred to thirteen thousand two hundred metres. We are one of five batteries in Division South West, we are part of the Quick Reaction Force on one hour's notice to move.

We deploy now and then in the Bosnian Serb area, the Bosnian Croat area and the Bosnian Muslim area, just to show our presence, showing our force and capabilities. The unit consists of one hundred and sixty men, no women, we've got fifteen APCs for ground moves and Mercedes jeeps with soft tops for air moves.

We are stationed in Jezero which is in the middle of the division area, so we can hop to all the places very quickly. Is that enough?"

## Perry Wells

### MAJOR, 2ND CANADIAN BRIGADE

### Interviewed at Canadian HQ, near Bihac

"We, as IFOR, provide the military security so that the civil agents can do their part – humanitarian aid, crimes and investigations, civil reconstruction, return of displaced people, law and order, democratic elections, regional stability – with the desire and hope that we can achieve peace here.

We salute the person who drafted the military portion of the peace agreement because there are very specific timelines laid down; D+45, D+90 and so on. It allows us to put this in front of the factions and hold them to a timeline. They are still soldiers and they understand soldierly things, and soldiers are big fans of timings. These are an important tool for us and they work well.

D+120 is a momentous task: the cantonment and demobilisation of the faction forces. It would be a monumentally difficult thing for us to do. We organise our military now and then, it takes years and we mess it up all the way along, and we're asking these people, who are not a professional army, to try and demobilise, and impose western staff standards that they didn't use throughout the war.

They're doing well at it – or they are really bullshitting us well. We're quite pleased with the 5th Corps in Bihac, they're genuinely doing the best they can and they appreciate our input and assistance to help them along. The small 101st HVO unit – it's easy for them, they're small. We're having more difficulties with the 1st Krajina Corps , a large area corps that reaches across the country, almost into the American sector. They're a bit more leery and anti-west and are having a bit more difficulty coming to grips with some of the things they're being asked to do.

Top.
A Dutch mortar crew on a live firing exercise at Glamoc. Holland uses large mortars instad of heavy artillery and these mortars, when rocket assisted, have an effective range of 13 kilometres.

Bottom.
The 120mm mortar shells that are used by the Dutch Army in Bosnia.

There are two thousand three hundred soldiers in our brigade and these include Americans, Dutch, British, Czechs, two New Zealanders and a Greek. Out of that total there are nine hundred and ninety two Canadian soldiers, our government limited us to a thousand troops here. Although they call us NATO our communications systems are incompatible, so we've had to provide communication detachments, of about ten to fifteen men each, to both the Czech and British brigades. We like the mandate, we like the force structure; we came in heavy.

One of the biggest NGOs in the Bihac area during the war was Care Canada, and so we are reaping some of the benefits. The only drawback is that because there's nothing dramatic going on, the media back home are not really tracking us too carefully. When we first got here there was a lot of interest but that has died right down.

There are three options for the future: peace breaks out and we all go home; partial success and something replaces us; peace fails and we leave. We anticipate that peace will partially succeed, the second option, and the public across the world is being sensitised to the idea of IFOR staying on."

## Brian McTavish

### PRIVATE, 2ND CANADIAN BRIGADE

#### Interviewed at Canadian HQ, near Bihac

"My dad put the idea in my head of joining the Army, he said it was a good idea and he gave me the papers. He had always wanted to join the Army but, at the time, he was too young. I'm one of the newest to the battalion and the first thing that happened when we arrived was the Sergeant Major took us on a ten kilometre run, he was pretty good and he wiped us into the ground.

When I first landed here I couldn't believe I was out of Canada, it was my first time. The countryside was beautiful but the towns all shot up. So, you go into the countryside and it's so beautiful and then you go back into the town – and this. It was a bit shocking at first but now it just flies over your head, you get used to it. It looks like it's getting better here. The cement factory here is working again and they're slowly rebuilding the country. IFOR's presence is a big part of the peace, if the UN were still here they would still be pushing, pushing. But we're not horsing around anymore.

As a driver you can be going down these long, windy roads and you come round a corner and there will be a big bus there – half on your side, half on his – really not paying attention to the road. You swerve out of the way – there's a mountain there and a cliff here, with a two foot play before it. When this happened to me I swerved right onto that edge and I still nicked him. Some of the driving here can be testing.

We're instructed to stay on the road. We've got a £32,000 (US$50,000) carrier, they've got a couple of hundred pound car and they try and force us off the roads. But we would rather take the chance with the car than with the mines so we stay on the hard pavement, usually in the middle of the road.

Sometimes they don't really mean it but other times they are on our side of the road. The drivers here will test you, they're a little crazy. They're not a defensive type of driver, they're an offensive type of driver, they just go for it. 'Who gives a damn' type of thing. We were told, 'Don't drive as crazy as them but when you've got to drive be aggressive,

Top left.
Michael Picard, a Private in the Canadian Army, inside his room at Brigade HQ, near Bihac.

Top middle.
Perry Wells, a Major in the Canadian Army outside the Brigade HQ, near Bihac.

Top right.
Brian McTavish, a private in the Canadian Army, inside his room at Brigade HQ, near Bihac.

Bottom.
A destroyed Mosque in the Canadian area of responsibility, near the extremist Serb town of Prijedor.

don't chicken out of anything.'

There have been two accidents right outside the main gate here. They're drunk or something, they just swerve into the ditch. The local police in this area have been monitoring the road, not extorting money just checking speeds and ID papers."

# Michael Picard

### PRIVATE, 2ND CANADIAN BRIGADE

### Interviewed at Canadian HQ, near Bihac

"I see the highlight of the tour working with the Czechs, I thought it was incredible. We've had a chance to see inside their BMP2, their armoured tracked vehicle, up close and it was amazing. Every last one of us dismounted carriers, exchanged weapons, totally wanted to see what the other had to show. The Czechs don't fool around, they don't take anything for granted. They hold their position firm and I think they're pretty good soldiers.

I was impressed when we did a joint patrol, and I think they were impressed with us because our Grizzly was the only wheeled vehicle in the whole convoy – there were four Warriors, two BMPs and only one Grizzly. At one point the Czech commander gave us an alternative route because he didn't feel we could get through the terrain in a wheeled vehicle. Our sergeant said, 'We can do it', and we made it pretty easily. It was a do or die situation.

We patrolled their area of responsibility and they led the patrol. But we kept losing the BMPs behind us and we couldn't figure out why. What they were doing was every time they passed a Serb or a Muslim bunker the guy would just ram the bunker with the BMP, totally destroying it. He would then pull back and the front was all covered in rocks and the lights were falling off. We would be going straight down the road and all of a sudden they would just slam right into the rock face."

## THE CZECHS

# Jiri Libal

### PRIVATE, CZECH BATTALION

**Interviewed at a village near Prijedor**

"I am from south Moravia and I joined the Army when I was fourteen. The Army has its own High Schools and I passed through Military High School, then Military Academy and then I came to Bosnia on the 2nd of February 1996. We were doing patrols from the third day of arrival, in the Zone of Separation. We would do a hundred to two hundred kilometres a day, checking upon houses, weapons, people. This is my first foreign mission, the first time I've seen destroyed, burned houses.

We destroy bunkers that are on our patrol route, we drive over them in the BMP – after we have searched it for mines and booby traps. The most interesting thing is looking for new patrol routes, standard patrol routes become boring. We were once surrounded by a rioting, furious mob when we were escorting a group of Muslims through a Serb area.

The BMP is much better in the terrain than the Warrior, much higher manoeuvrability and the weapons system is better. The only thing that's better in the Warrior is the optical devices. Those British soldiers who had the opportunity of seeing the BMP, of comparing, would agree with this. General Jeffries, the Commander of the Second Brigade, had the opportunity of seeing the BMP on the live firing exercise. He shot from the BMP and every shot hit the target. He proclaimed the BMP an excellent vehicle with good weapon systems. It is made in Russia.

> Local people think that as soon as IFOR leave, the war will start again, they're afraid. I've also met people who are disgusted with IFOR, they say we're occupying their country and we should get out.

The AK-47 is very simple, we call it 'Soldier proof' You can't destroy it. Compared to the SA-80 used by the British it is very easy to disassemble, it's very good in bad conditions, dusty environments – if you have sand in the weapon it still shoots. We can't say that about the SA-80. In case there's something wrong with the weapon you can disassemble it very quickly, it's accurate and very handy with the folding shoulder rest.

By comparison, the M16 is very complicated and sensitive to dust and sand. Recently, we received night vision devices from the Czech Republic that are better than the ones of the other countries. Our general opinion is that we've got better equipment than the other units here.

Local people think that as soon as IFOR, leave the war will start again, they're afraid. I've also met people who are disgusted with IFOR, they say we're occupying their country and we should get out."

# Josef Proks

## LIEUTENANT COLONEL, COMMANDER OF CZECH BATTALION

### Interviewed at Czech HQ at Ljubija, near Prijedor

"The Army in the Czech Republic is not so popular among the civilians. Despite this, our contribution to IFOR enhances our reputation among civilians. The Army view of this mission is very positive. This is the first, non-UN, foreign mission for the Czech Army.

Since leaving the Warsaw Pact there has been a great reorganisation of the Army. Armies that were formerly presented as enemies were suddenly able to do joint exercises with us. For me, this was amazing. Co-operation was always very good, especially at the platoon and company level. Language has been a problem but we added interpreters to each unit and, if soldiers want to co-operate and make friends, language is not the main problem.

Before, in the Warsaw Pact, we were orientated against NATO countries and so all our bases were deployed in a way to react to an enemy coming from the west. It fell, such a threat fell, and we had to relocate, re-deploy and reorganise on the basis of protecting our country from all directions.

We had to destroy a lot of weapons and move a lot of people from one location to another. It took a lot of time and effort. We have opened new branches of the Army – logistics, medical, finance – and also changed our style of work. The Warsaw Pact way of working limited us so much that everyone sees the benefits of working in this new way.

The main change of style was that in the Army we had a centralised command system and commanders, even at high levels, were not allowed to make their own decisions. The top commander would control everything. Now, commanders at low levels have much more rights to make decisions. It's lighter to breathe in our country now we are free.

I was nine years old in 1968, but the events of that year affected everything. The main change for the Army was that before '68 we were commanded by the Russian command post for the whole of the Warsaw Pact countries, but after '68 they deployed around one hundred thousand Soviet troops in our country, and of course put us under their direct military command. This drastically affected the balance of force in Central Europe. Of course people were not happy with the situation but gradually we got used to it and made friends at a personal level. But, as a foreign body in our country, they were never accepted. Nobody was happy about their presence in our country.

It was the behaviour of the Russians that created the opinion of the people and this was largely formed by the environmental problems. Because they had a lot of fuel, big leaks occurred in our forests, they destroyed large areas. We can find unexploded ordnance everywhere: mines, projectiles, everything. They had control of large areas of the Czech Republic, areas that were only accessible to the Russians. Now they have left and now our kids, our civilians, find large quantities of unexploded bombs in dangerous areas, mostly spoilt areas.

We are not a rich country but we are a modern country with a very rich culture. If you want to learn something about the Czech Republic the best way is to visit the country."

Czech BMP-2
patrolling the
Zone of Separation
in the hills above
Prijedor, western Bosnia.

# The French Division and Civil Affairs

## THE FRENCH BRIGADE

# George Ladeveze

BRIGADIER GENERAL, COMMANDER OF FRENCH BRIGADE

### Interviewed at French HQ, Sarajevo

"Initially, the French contingent were observers, then troops of the UN and now they are IFOR. I think public opinion is positively behind our efforts to find a solution for this country, and I think this is now accepted in France. Under UNPROFOR it was very complicated and I wonder if the people in France were able to understand, exactly, the mission here. But the IFOR mission is very clear and, I think, well accepted.

We have three thousand five hundred French soldiers here now. Although we are not a full member of NATO, we have no real problems with them now that we work within the NATO structure. It has become easier and easier to work together.

Since World War Two this is the first time that all developed countries have worked together – this is very important. Of course we have some language problems; some people say that French people are not very good at languages – and they are right. But, I can tell you, that in the last ten years we have been working very hard to oblige every officer, and most of the NCOs, and when we can, our soldiers, to speak at least English and, if possible, another language.

English language is being developed in the French Army and, mostly among the young people, there is not a single officer who is not able to say sufficient words – mainly for technical things. Also, they are developing their general knowledge of English and American culture. We have good relations with the Italian Brigade, our northern neighbours, and the Spanish Brigade, our southern neighbours.

I have the Ukrainian Battalion under my command and the Ukrainians were a surprise to me; I found them very clever, very nice people. Here, I have five Ukrainian Liaison Officers who speak very good French, they work very seriously and exactly in the way I want. It's a great pleasure to have them under my command. They are very professional.

This is my fifth time in operations – formerly I was in Lebanon, Saudi Arabia and Kuwait. Here I was struck by the quietness of the situation, but it's an evolving situation. There is freedom of movement but people do not dare to use it. We are sure that nothing bad can happen but I don't think the people are aware of this. We will be highly involved in the elections as we were in Mostar, where we learned to keep our distance from the polling booths.

Our view of the Americans is very positive. In history we worked a lot together; first, two centuries ago, we helped them to be independent. Now they come back each time we need them. Recently, in the Gulf War, we worked very closely with them, it is very easy. I have a lot of American, British, German, Italian and Spanish friends here. The most interesting part of this way of working is that you can appreciate the role of everybody,

> I think public opinion is positively behind our efforts to find a solution for this country, and I think this is now accepted in France.

Previous page.
British infantry soldier in Bugojno

This Page, top.
Brigadier General George Ladeveze,
Commander of the French
Brigade, Sarajevo airport.

Bottom.
Italian tank park in Sarajevo.
The Italian Army provide the
heavy armour for the
French Division.

Overleaf.
View of Sarajevo, the
capital city of Bosnia-Herzegovina,
from the old Turkish Fort.

every nation. We are learning a lot from the professional point of view here, we are becoming more and more able to work together."

## Pascal Henry Fritsch

### CAPTAIN, PUBLIC INFORMATION OFFICER
### 2ND FRENCH BATTALION

**Interviewed at Sarajevo Airport**

"If you want to knock the top off a champagne bottle you swing your sabre at it with an upward motion, you swing it so it comes up and catches the top of the bottle. The difficulty is the flick of the wrist. Get it right and the top comes off very neatly. I can do it with my sabre – all French officers have a sabre.

I am a generalist. It is a long tradition in the Army – whatever the job, an officer can do it. I began in the paratroopers. I joined them because I decided they were the best. At the time, I thought the world was one big dropzone. Then I decided I wanted to become an officer. I moved to tanks, I commanded a platoon, four tanks. It is a good feeling, all that firepower, big power. Then they were looking for a PIO (Press Information Officer) and Civil Affairs Officer and they decided on me.

I arrived in February, with my unit from its base in Germany. I live there with my wife and young son, Jeremy, who is now ten months old. If you want to have peace there have to be soldiers. If there is fighting then we are going to fight.

Whenever a journalist comes out I take them around the different units in the battalion. It's interesting work, I get to see a great deal. One thing I can see is that everyone has a different perspective on what is happening. Sometimes a journalist will come here with an idea ready formed of how things are. They will come wanting to find people who conform to that view. If they want to find poor people, they will find poor people. Regional journalists are interested by what our soldiers are doing, national journalists not so much. They are interested in the overall picture. I prefer working with regional journalists.

The important thing in this job is to always remain calm. Working with journalists is a chess game – you have to be ahead of the next question. And you have to be very careful when dealing with journalists – the record is never off !"

> Working with journalists is a chess game – you have to be ahead of the next question.

Top.
A Turkish member of the IPTF (International Task Police Force) walks past two Bosnian waitresses outside their cafe in central Sarajevo.

Bottom.
Christian Colonette, a captain in the French Army and interpreter at Brigade HQ, Sarajevo airport.

## Didier Jaegle

### HEAD CHEF, 2ND FRENCH BRIGADE

**Interviewed at Sarajevo Airport**

"My day starts at 7am. Half the cooks have breakfast before making breakfast for everyone else, and the other half afterwards. We work in teams of two, two do the meat, two the vegetables.

Then there is the cleaning, we have to clean everything, the pots and big ovens, twice a day. There is a once a week inspection. We sometimes work after dinner time, we might have to do late dinners too. If a company is on a mission and comes in late, they have to have a hot meal. It is a long day, we take breaks when we can. We get only one day off a month. Saturdays are easier, we only have to prepare salads, each soldier gets a ration pack for those meals.

My task is cooking for the staff – the headquarters staff eat separately from the infantry companies. Because this is the airport base there are often guests, VIPs sometimes. Dinner is one main course, with a choice of hors d'oeuvres and salads – lots of salad. Vegetarians are very rare among French troops – we serve thirteen hundred people and just two them are vegetarians.

For the French it's important to have food of a high standard. You can survive on ration packs but when you have the choice it is better to have good food. For troops on long tours, food is very important. It is also important to give soldiers familiar food. For instance the US soldiers, they expect familiar foods, pizza or hamburgers. It's important to them when they're away from home. And it's the same for the French. We do a good job. We don't get complaints, except from some for the Muslims. They complain because when we have a dish with pork, although we do provide an alternative, they complain it's always the same alternative.

But we do a good job. At the ARRC headquarters in Sarajevo, it's usually the British who do the cooking but for these special occasions they had to bring in the French. They wanted a special cake in the shape of a crocodile and only we had the skills. We have patisserie specialists who are trained to produce anything you can find in any patisserie in Paris.

Special occasions are very important – regimental days, the colonel's birthday, or Bastille Day. Special events break the monotony of a long tour. It's important for the soldier and it's important for the chefs. We do special meals – we had lobster for Bastille Day. And we made a huge cake for the regimental day – it took 18 hours for our patisserie chef. He made the regimental logo in icing. There's another reason these occasions are important. They give a chance for everyone on the base to come together at the same time. That's very important.

I was always interested in cooking. By the time of my National Service at eighteen, I had a cookery diploma from High School. So when I was drafted I was put in the kitchen. Then I signed on for the Regular Army, that was in March 1988. I plan to stay in the Army another five years. Then I'll be thirty three, that's a good age to leave. You get plenty of experience in the army, but you're young enough to start something new.

I plan to open a restaurant in France specialising in Alsace cuisine: pies, sauerkraut, salad du cervelas, that sort of thing. I'm going to open it with my wife Sylviane. She is also an army chef, in fact she's senior to me in rank, but at home we're equal.

We don't go out of the base except on missions, so I don't meet ordinary Bosnians. The only Bosnians I meet are the girls we hire to help in the kitchens. The battalion policy is to hire them from all ethnic groups, and in fact none of us in the kitchen know who is from which ethnic group. I do guard duty, everyone on the base does. We are soldiers first and cooks second."

> They wanted a special cake in the shape of a crocodile and only we had the skills. We have patisserie specialists who are trained to produce anything you can find in any patisserie in Paris.

An Italian soldier in Sarajevo wearing the distinctive camouflage that represents membership of the Bersaglieri Corps.

# Christian Colonette

CORPORAL, INTERPRETER, 2ND FRENCH BATTALION

### Interviewed at Sarajevo Airport

"I graduated from Martinique University in English and Mathematics. I always thought that my ten months of service would be a time when I would think about what I would do in the future. Martinique is a Department (region) of France and I could have done my military service there, but I wanted to spend these ten months far from my home. So I went to France. I was sent to my unit, the 19 Chausseurs (Cavalry) in February of this year in Schwarzwald, Germany.

On the first day in Germany they said, 'if you want, there may be the possibility of going to Bosnia'. I was totally surprised. I thought, 'Oh my God, I'm only doing my draft'. I volunteered. The closer we were to the departure date, the more people wanted to go.

My father was with the French CRS (French Riot Police) forces in Algeria many years ago. He had told me, 'If they tell you to go to Bosnia say no, no, no.' I remember when I told him I'm going to Bosnia, he said, 'Are you crazy?' But that's changed, now he's saying it's good. My motivation for going to Bosnia was that it is interesting. Here, we are in the place of history. Afterwards, we will be able to say, 'We were there'. Dying doesn't worry me. I've studied mathematics, probabilities. It might be dangerous but you always have a chance to die – you might die crossing the road."

# Don Claudio

PADRE, ITALIAN PARACHUTE BRIGADE FOLGORE

Top.
The River Neretva running through the divided city of Mostar. The hill in the background was held by the HVO (Bosnian Croat Army) and used as a mortar firing position to shell this ancient city; note the fortified gun emplacement at the top of the hill.

Bottom.
A West Mostar Mafia leader flies the Croat flag in provocation to Muslims on Mostar's east side, during the Mostar local elections. The French anti sniper team in the background helped maintain public order, and this particular local hood was soon moved on.

### Interviewed at Italian Brigade HQ at Sarajevo

"When I was a child I liked the image of the Catholic Church. As I grew older I realised this was what I wanted to do with my life. I started as a Parish Priest, first at Grezzana, near Verona, then later at Manerba del Garda, in Lombardy. While I was there I often met young people who were doing military service and they told me there weren't enough chaplains. So in 1990 I joined the Military Chaplaincy.

The way it is in Italy is that I am still a member of the Italian Church – in effect I am borrowed from the church by the Army. When I first became a chaplain I did a fifteen day training course, learning about the structure of the army, the ranks and so on, and official procedures. Then I was assigned to the Paratroopers. I can do more training if I want to; I can do parachute jumps. The only thing I have no involvement with is firearms.

My day starts like anybody else's. I get up at seven and I say prayers until eight when there is a flag raising ceremony. Then I tour the base. I visit all the rooms, the places where the soldiers live, the infirmary, the kitchen, the bunkers where the soldiers are on guard, and I ask how things are. If they have problems they can talk about them. They can be shy – the big soldiers or the small soldiers. People don't look for you but if sometimes I fail to pass by their place one day then the day after they say, 'Why didn't you come?'

I hold a lot of services. Because the troops are dispersed, I visit the different bases. There are services every day, in the afternoon. On Sunday I do two, one at the Tito

Barracks in central Sarajevo, and again at twelve at Zetra, the main base. On Saturday mornings I hold a service for the soldiers at the artillery deployment. Some of the soldiers are studying for confirmation so I also give them religious instruction.

We have a programme of long distance adoption here: soldiers, individually or in groups, can adopt an orphan. For every six hundred Deutschmarks we raise we can pay for an orphan to be looked after for a year. It is not adoption in the formal sense – it is more like sponsorship. The soldiers make a link with the child. But it may be in the future that some of these children can be adopted by families in Europe. The soldiers are keen on doing this: sometimes a company pools its money to adopt a child, sometimes an individual soldier will do it. There is a great problem in Sarajevo with orphans because the orphanage was destroyed in the war. I also keep links with the Catholic church here in Sarajevo.

In June I joined the military pilgrimage to Lourdes. It is the third time I've been on this. It takes place early in the month. There were fourteen thousand soldiers from twenty four nations. The Italian soldiers here are religious. Everybody asks for a cross to put on their wall, and many also ask for bibles. I am a sort of reference point – a link between the commander and the soldiers. I can guage their morale and tell him how they feel.

Top.
A Bosnian woman finds her way through the rubble of a former frontline between Croat and Muslim held Mostar. A Spanish Armoured Personnel Carrier watches over a street that was a no-man's land for the last few years and has only recently opened to pedestrians.

Bottom.
Spanish BMR-600 Armoured Personnel Carrier on patrol in Mostar's Boulevard. This street was the former front line between the Croat and Muslim sides of Mostar.

## THE ROMANIAN ROADBUILDERS

# Viorel Gurau

MAJOR, ROMANIAN ENGINEERING BATTALION

### Interviewed on road to Gorazde

"We are engineers, not fighters. Two hundred engineers came here to build roads and bridges and do de-mining operations. We have built four bridges so far, including the longest bridge, in Doboj, built since the end of the war, and now we're building eleven kilometres of road in the Gorazde corridor.

We were the only IFOR contingent that was willing to start work on the Kosevo Olympic Stadium in Sarajevo. I don't know why the other Armies weren't interested – probably because the terrain had been turned into hundreds of gardens by the people, but our Commander thought it was an interesting job.

At the Kosevo Stadium we completed the first stage of the job which involved moving over four thousand cubic metres of earth, digging out the area and then levelling an area of eighteen hundred metres in three weeks. Now, a private Italian firm is finishing off the final stages of the job.

We feel good here and always we have wanted to prove that we are a good army, even though, compared to other armies, we do not have sufficient equipment. However, we are able to do the mission and everything has been done on schedule and to a high quality – as good as anybody.

It seems normal that we want to do more than everybody else and we are very interested in learning from the other armies here. This whole mission has been an extraordinary thing for us, we're delighted to be here and we like it very much."

# Dan Arsenescu

NCO, ROMANIAN ENGINEERING BATTALION

### Interviewed at Base Camp on road to Gorazde

"The Army is a unique and different structure to all others in Romania. We have an order and discipline that does not exist in other institutions where corruption has made itself felt. Our Army has a long tradition and I have served in Somalia with the UN, where we ran a field hospital and I learned what it was like to work with 135 different countries. Somalia wasn't our first mission under the UN, there was also Angola.

This corridor road to Gorazde is a very difficult job. It goes through a very narrow, steep valley that is completely uninhabited; our camp is the only thing here. The existing road is very narrow, only three metres wide, and isn't large enough for trucks. We're blasting rocks and digging the road to a width of six metres, also we're going to make spaces for checkpoints.

We have really dirty hard work but we enjoy it. A lot of it we do by hand because the

Top.
Romanian engineers work at widening the 'corridor' road to Gorazde. This road cuts a thin line through a Serb dominated sector of south-east Bosnia to the Muslim enclave of Gorazde. It would be almost imposible to defend this road should the Serbs decide to cut it off.

Bottom.
Major Viorel Gurau, Commander of the Romanian Engineering Company on the road to Gorazde, shows a Romanian-made water filtration system.

Overleaf.
Members of the Romanian Engineering Battalion pose for the camera on their Armoured Personel Carrier, Zenica.

141

road is too narrow to work with the proper equipment. We have sixty people working here. We are trying to add something to IFOR and also to make something for our country. We want to be able to get out and join NATO.

We go to work without guns and firepower because we want to create a good impression with the local community, we want to make friends with everybody."

## Ilie Lupu

### MAJOR, ROMANIAN ENGINEERING BATTALION

**Interviewed on road to Gorazde**

"After the Romanian Revolution in December 1989, the Army, alongside the Church, remained as the most credible institution. The role of the Army is the defence of the Borders. We have Catholics and Orthodox and other religions in our country but we don't have a problem with that.

> We've got some good soldiers here and they're doing the job very well because they're driven by a will to do things better than the others.

We came here to work, that was the main reason, but also to demonstrate that we are in a suitable state to become a member of NATO. We've got some good soldiers here and they're doing the job very well because they're driven by a will to do things better than the others.

All the equipment we have here is Romanian, all built by Romanian industry: graders, bulldozers, heavy trucks, jeeps, armoured personnel carriers, mechanical shovels. Although there was scepticism at first, this equipment has performed well and it has proved to be compatible – it hasn't made us look like fools. I'm not sure that there is any other country that produces all their own equipment as we do.

The DAC truck has been particularly impressive out here, it hasn't got stuck anywhere and I don't think it could get stuck anywhere. You won't see any Romanian vehicles broken down by the side of the road. All we want to show is reality; we want the other countries to judge us on what we have done, nothing else. We have very hardworking and clever people who have performed as well as any other member state of NATO."

Top.
Romanian earth-moving equipment tests its mettle by working on the 'corridor' road to Gorazde.

Bottom left.
Romanian logistician Dan Arsenescu, at the Romanian road camp on the road to Gorazde.

Bottom right.
Brady Bluhm, of the United States Air Force, stationed with the Romanian road building team on the road to Gorazde to provide Close Air Support.

## Brady Bluhm

### SENIOR AIRMAN, USAF (UNITED STATES AIR FORCE)

**Interviewed on road to Gorazde**

"I've been here about a month now in this camp with the Romanians, we're here as liaison to provide CAS (Close Air Support). They're very down to earth, very good people, they've pretty much taken us under their wings and treated us like family. It's been nice. I was here with the Pakistanis before and they kept us away from everyone. With the Romanians it's the total opposite.

They're very hard workers; they work until night and get round the obstacles. I've been very surprised what hard charging people they are. It's similar to the road construction

crews back home but these guys are out all the time. It's something I wouldn't want to do, that's why I'm in the Air Force.

The Romanians want to show the world that they are hard workers and that they want to be part of NATO. They've made a good impression so far and everyone wants to come and work with them in this camp up here. All the other guys I'm with come up here as much as possible to be around the Romanians – the food is great and they really take care of you.

Everyone teases the Air Force because they've got a pretty good life, the chow halls are good, the Air Force treats its people good. I could dog on the Army because they get shit on, but that's just the army way of life. They don't get the good equipment like the Air Force does. They make fun of us because we get to go to places and live in a hotel rather than out in the mud, but I'd rather live in a hotel than out in the mud and stuff.

> All the other guys I'm with come up here as much as possible to be around the Romanians – the food is great and they really take care of you.

## Tony Vladu

### SPECIAL FORCES ENGINEER, US ARMY

**Interviewed at Romanian Camp on road to Gorazde**

"I was born in 1971 in Romania and my family went to the United States in 1984. It took my mother five years of protesting and complaining before the Romanian authorities would let us leave legally. Maybe my parents felt the oppression under Communism in Romania but I didn't, I was far too busy going to school and having fun. I was having lots of fun.

I was impressed with the schools in Romania. In the sixth grade I was taking physics, and by the fourth grade I was doing Russian. In the States it took about a year to learn the language, they put us in an English as a Second Language class and there were people there from all over the world. New York is a pretty diverse town, and then it was all downhill from there.

As an example of how high the education system in Romania was, they put us two grades higher and even there I was scoring much higher in maths than the other kids. In the States a lot of people haven't even heard of Romania, maybe two out of ten have heard of it. I've only met two or three people who know where it is, and that's because they've lived there, the others think its a suburb of Rome or somewhere in Africa.

The reason a lot of people don't know what Romania is all about is that it's an island of Latin people – because the Romans took it over, in the middle of a Slavic area. The people are very different, very warm, you can compare them to the Spanish or Italian people.

It's just like being home here, there are people here who lived on the same street as me. The hospitality is great, we've been here a month but it seems like we've just been here a few days. They're doing really good here; it's a really difficult job as it's easier to build a new road than build on an existing road. And there are nine bridges in an eleven kilometre stretch, this is probably the hardest bit."

Tony Vladu, Special Forces engineer, based with Romanian Engineering Battalion on the road to Gorazde.

Overleaf, left page Townspeople in Gorazde fishing in the River Drina; Gorazde is the last of the Bosnian Government-held enclaves in Serb dominated eastern Bosnia.

Right page.
Top.
Bosnian soldiers play football on the road to Gorazde, which is possible because the road is so bad that few people use it

Bottom.
Visegrad town, near Gorazde. This Turkish-built bridge was immortalised in the Nobel prize winning novel **The Bridge over the Drina.**

# US ARMY CIVIL AFFAIRS TEAM

## Dealing with the People

## Semir Softic

TRANSLATOR WITH CIVIL AFFAIRS TEAM

### Interviewed at Camp Diane

"I first came to Camp Diane in February, it was night time and it was snowing. All the camp was in mud to the knees, mud everywhere. The captain took us to a truck with food and we had to eat standing in the mud up to the knees, in the snow. It was so cold it was incredible. I was thinking, 'Oh God, I should go home'. But I was lucky because Captain Scott Miller took me in when I started to work for the Civil Affairs Team.

My first job was to go to the Serbian village of Palamic, and I'd never been on Serb territory before that. The Bosnian Army had taken that village about two years ago and unfortunately the Bosnian Army had destroyed all the houses. The Serbs were really mad about it and they took back that village. And, on my first day, I had to go back to that village and talk with the Serbs.

I didn't feel very well that time. I didn't know Americans and I was remembering UNPROFOR when some Serbs had arrested some translators. I had to tell my Captain, 'Please call me Sam, not Samir, just Sam', and from that time on they call me Sam. It was foggy, we were going between the minefields, there were big warning signs everywhere. We didn't find any Serbs there and we had to come back to the base.

The first time I met Serbs was in Sekovici. They were surprised to meet me, to meet a Muslim. But actually they asked me about some friends of theirs in Tuzla, some cousins of theirs, and they asked how it was in Tuzla. I was surprised, nicely surprised, it was good meeting with them, it wasn't provocative. Sometimes we take letters from Serbs to Muslims, and from Muslims to Serbs.

On the street in Sekovici I met a kid who had come from Sarajevo ten days earlier, when the Serbs had to leave Sarajevo in Bosnian hands. I asked him, 'Why did you come here? Why didn't you stay in Sarajevo?' And that kid, about ten years old, answered me, 'Oh, I was afraid that the Turkish people would kill me'. 'What Turkish people?' I answered, 'Where are the Turkish people? We aren't Turkish people, we are Bosnians.' But he was a kid and he was growing up with big propaganda.

On the Serb side we haven't had any bad experiences, most of them said they didn't want war again, actually that they shouldn't have had war. The point is that most of the people there are normal, but it seems that high policy made everything.

Usually our job is dealing with damage claims, we go and assess what damage IFOR made in the local communities. The Americans do this job very well, very diligently, they really try and help people. If we have a mission we usually get up at six in the morning and go to another base to get in a four vehicle convoy. The roads are very bad, many holes, but when we go through the villages most people treat us like heroes, especially the children. On the Bosnian and the Serb sides they accept us very well.

One day an old man came to the gate and asked for a hearing aid. I was surprised that he came to IFOR, we are soldiers and we don't need those machines, we don't have them.

Semir 'Sam' Softic, the Bosnian translator for the 2nd Brigade Civil Affairs team. Sam is based in Camp Diane.

The captain came and answered him, 'Soldiers who can't hear can't be soldiers'. That captain left three months ago, and last week he sent us a hearing aid for that man. We visited the old man and gave him that present and he was very surprised and very satisfied. It's really nice to help people, although IFOR's job is not to help people in that way.

Before the war, in former Yugoslavia, it was a habit to work approximately four hours a day, a maximum of four hours a day, although the work time was eight hours. Workers were drinking alcohol on the job, it was the normal thing, from manual workers to university professors. It was normal to go to the professors and see them sitting there drinking, and talking. We had really bad habits; but here it's absolutely different. We had all watched American movies you know, with many American heroes. I thought all Americans were like aliens, like beings from other planets. But they are actually emotional people like we are, actually they're very similar to how we are. I especially didn't expect to have such good friends like I have with American soldiers.

In the first days I thought maybe some of the soldiers were gay. Me and Baci (the Serb translator at Camp Diane) both thought so, we were afraid and we were talking dirty things to each other like we were macho guys, saying, 'You dirty sonofabitch, you lazy motherfucker', bad things so that the soldiers would think, 'What macho guys!' But really, I'm glad I was wrong. In movies every American has got a few females, or they are divorced and have lovers. But most of them are faithful people. It was incredible for me, I didn't believe them. But really they are, especially the people who believe in God and go to prayers here. They're really faithful, only one woman – nothing more.

The first day I saw Baci, the Serb translator, I was sick when I heard his voice because I knew that all this war came from Belgrade and he was from Belgrade. But, from that time on, I saw that he's a really nice guy, a very interesting guy and I think everything the best about him. He was in the USA for two years and he's very, very clever. It's really nice to work with him. We share the same room, the same job. Sometimes we talk about politics and he was surprised, very surprised, when he saw that on the Bosnian side there are Serbs. He didn't know it because of the propaganda. He was thinking that here it is something like Iran and he didn't know what the local Serbs from Republika Srpska actually did here, especially about the massacre in Tuzla.

The first time he was in Tuzla Airbase he was talking to some Serbs who live in Tuzla city, free people. He didn't believe that there were free people with rights on the Bosnian side. He was thinking it was just the Muslim side. He saw the church in Kladanj, an unspoilt church, and he met some Serbs in Kladanj who were in the Bosnian Army. When he had his first days off, he was talking to some Serbs in Belgrade about the situation here and they told him, 'You are a Fundamentalist'.

The former Yugoslavia was the United States of the eastern part of Europe. It was the best. We had much more freedom than other east European countries. We actually had too much freedom, more than we deserved. It was impossible to be fired, impossible to fire some workers. Only political freedom wasn't so big, but in other ways we were really free people, you could sleep anywhere in former Yugoslavia; in the car, woods, forest, on the coast.

> We had all watched American movies you know, with many American heroes. I thought all Americans were like aliens, like beings from other planets. But they are actually emotional people like we are, actually they're very similar to how we are.

Top.
One of the jobs of the US Army Civil Affairs team is to conduct weapons inspections at declared weapons storage sites, or cantonment areas. When undertaking this high risk inspection, the armoured escort maintains a high profile. In this visit the M1A1 Main Battle Tank was parked in the the main gate.

Bottom.
The Civil Affairs team look for undeclared weapons in a Bosnian Serb 'Cantonment Area' where weapons are stored.

But people were drinking, they didn't do their job like they should do. Tito gave them maybe too many rights, but it happened. During Tito's time we were really like paradise. I suppose the safest country in the world with the lowest level of crime. It was a really nice country, almost the whole of Europe was coming to our Adriatic seaside. And we were like brothers, all nationalities, I had really big friends with Serbs and Croats. Before the war I was studying Mining Engineering at Tuzla City University. Tuzla was the biggest mining centre in former Yugoslavia. I graduated during the war and I hope that when I finish my job with IFOR I will start to do my job.

During the war I was in the Bosnian Army, in ordnance, heavy artillery. We had very few barrels and most of the time we didn't have enough shells, so most of the time we were unengaged. What artillery we did have was captured from the Serbs, stolen, but what we had was nothing compared to the Serbs. In the first two years it was a ratio of one of our shells to a hundred of theirs, it was incredible. And when we started to attack Serb soldiers they started with heavy artillery to beat our towns and to kill our civilians, and so we had to stop. This was a Serb habit, all around Bosnia-Herzegovina when we started to attack soldiers they started with heavy artillery to beat towns and civilians. That's why you can see all around Bosnia destroyed towns, that's the reason.

1993 was really the hardest year because it was war with the Serbs and the Croats, we were fighting against two enemies, two fronts. We were surrounded and it was a miracle that we didn't lose the war. Maybe it was because we were absolutely desperate and we didn't have anything else to lose, we were like Kamikaze maybe. That's why they didn't beat us."

## Timothy Joseph Krawczel

MAJOR, US ARMY RESERVE
CIVIL AFFAIRS TEAM LEADER WITH 2ND BRIGADE

### Interviewed at Camp Diane

"I'm from the Washington DC area but right now I'm living in a little town called Rocky Mount, Virginia. I've been in the Army nearly twenty years. I got out of graduate school and I had a masters degree in Urban Planning. I was looking around for work and couldn't get a job for a long time, so I said, 'I've got to do something, I've got to get started', and since then I've sort of grown into Civil Affairs, the branch that's closest to what I do in my civilian career. As a member of the Army Reserve it's pretty compatible.

I'm a Director of Planning and Community Development and do long range planning for county governments and municipalities. The basic problem you deal with in community development is making sure that the parties least able to take care of themselves have some basic level of social participation, access and opportunity to the social and economic life of the community.

The fundamental problem here in Bosnia, from one perspective, is a breakdown of life in the community and the inability of the different groups to participate with one another. People look at each other and decide there's a difference based upon social or ethnic characteristics that is more important than all the similarities they share. The people here strike me as being very handsome people – the way they carry themselves, the tall stature, the facial characteristics. They're a beautiful race of people in general.

Top.
An American soldier stands guard during an inspection of a Bosnian Serb weapons storage site, near Vlasnica.

Bottom.
The Civil Affairs team inspecting AK47's in an officially declared Bosnian Serb 'Cantonment Area'; these are designated sites for storing precise numbers of weapons and are open to inspection at any time by IFOR personnel.

Before I was in the Army I spent two and a half years in the Peace Corps. When I got out of college in 1969 I spent two and a half years in Nicaragua, an under-developed country. It had a tremendous impact on me; I totally assimilated and internalised the culture of the people and probably thought and acted more like a Nicaraguan than an American. So it was a tremendous jolt going back to the States.

We work for the 4-12 Task Force Commander and he has an area of operation of one thousand square kilometres with one hundred and twenty five thousand people in it, with four or five major towns – we are his representatives to the local community. If there are problems that arise with IFOR it's our job to deal with them; to make the stay of the 4-12 as compatible as possible with the social and economic life of the community. It is our intent to fulfil the military mission but to interfere as little as possible in the economic and social life of the community. I think it's been very effective.

At heart I think the Serb people just love the military. Everybody considers himself, or herself, a soldier in many ways and I think Serbians intuitively understand and accept IFOR in a lot of ways. I've noticed a genuine and positive response among the Serbian population to IFOR in the rural areas. Now, there are places where it's tainted by political propaganda or demagoguery, but the person living in the rural areas that I see really appreciates that we are here. The Bosnian Muslim population, who feel they were getting pounded by the Serbs, are thankful to the point of rejoicing almost.

We work with the International Police Task Force, God bless their hearts, up in Vlasnica – the little Russian fellow and the fellows from Africa. I have to admire them. I think they're very brave to sit out there in their stations with the history of what happened in this country and what happened to their predecessors; to sit out there in an unarmed, very vulnerable state and try to work with the civilian police and population, and conduct a training mission and a monitoring mission.

> At heart I think the Serb people just love the military. Everybody considers himself, or herself, a soldier in many ways and I think Serbians intuitively understand and accept IFOR in a lot of ways.

We've been going out recently surveying the response of people to the polling places and the response of some of them has been extraordinary. For example the Election Committee at Sahovici, where we expected a very hard line, with them being rigid and difficult to work with. We found them to be the nicest group of people that I've encountered yet; people that are working without any pay whatever, probably haven't had any job in four years, are enthusiastic and trying their darndest to have a good election, to get a good turnout and to follow and obey all the rules of the OSCE (Organisation for Security and Co-operation in Europe).

We said to them 'How do you feel about the election?' and they said 'Do you really want to know?' We said yes, and braced ourselves. They said, 'It's the greatest thing that has ever happened around here', and I think that was a genuine response, they weren't just saying what they wanted us to hear.

I listen and talk with the refugee families from the war that are still living in Refugee Centres. I remember a particular woman of forty five years old, with five or six kids, sitting in a Refugee Centre. I could almost picture her sitting by the fields and I intimately understood her realm of activity: she lives in a little village, she has lived there all her life; she has her fields to tend, her kids to raise and probably her parents live somewhere nearby and her grandparents are probably buried somewhere nearby, she may or may not

A crack appears on a road in Kladanj; a member of the Civil Affairs team looks into it. One of the jobs of Civil Affairs is to assess damage claims and pay compensation when IFOR have damaged civilian property.

have a couple of grand-children. She has all the social knowledge of the village; how to work and operate and she probably has the survival skills to bring in the crops and feed and sustain her family from one year to the next. You see what the war has done to that person long term. This person no longer has a husband, no longer has any male children, doesn't know where her father is, has lost all the male members of her family, her whole future and that of her children is just totally destroyed.

She doesn't have a village to go back to, she doesn't have any land that she owns, she doesn't have anybody that earns a livelihood, but she still has those kids. How is she going to survive the next one, two, three years? How is she going to support her family? Who is going to provide long term shelter for her and her children? Who wants that kind of responsibility? She is totally displaced from everything that she knows. That impact of the war, the enormous long term effect of war on the social fabric of society, has been incredible.

I think what happens depends on the quality of leadership. I'm not at all impressed by the quality of leadership of the Serbian or Muslim people – if they fail to establish peace, that is the reason why. It seems like Karadzic has a death grip in the minds and on the future of the Serb people. He's somebody who cannot lead them into the future, cannot work with the international community, cannot bring resources or progress into the country. Yet he has this grip on the aspirations of the people and until he's replaced by five or ten people, who are keen to open up opportunities for the people and linkages with other countries and social groups, there won't be any real progress. People seem happy to just sit there with this clamp on the arteries that bring nourishment to the country. That has to be changed; there have to be new leaders that have new ideas and not just building their power base on old hatreds.

There are a lot of groups that will tell you that working with Muslim dominated cultures is tough anywhere, it takes pretty skilful business and political leaders to do that, it's not an easy job. Looking on the horizon we certainly don't see the right kind of leadership. I just don't see the skill or level of applied intelligence that it takes, that has to emerge and I just don't see it happening."

> It seems like Karadzic has a death grip in the minds and on the future of the Serb people. He's somebody who cannot lead them into the future, cannot work with the international community, cannot bring resources or progress into the country.

# Roderick Anderson

### PRIVATE, US ARMY, 4-12 INFANTRY

**Interviewed while on guard duty at Camp Diane**

"I think this deployment is really good because we're really making a change, for the kids especially, they have a future to look forward to. I've just left Fort Bragg, the 101st Airborne, but I come from Mississippi. At Fort Bragg you're on two hour recall and you've got to be ready to deploy within twenty four hours.

I went to Haiti for two months and it was nice, a big change. Some people didn't like us being there and, like here, there were people who couldn't wait for us to leave. Since I've been here I've seen a lot of improvements. I've seen more people travelling, more

Top.
Roderick Anderson maintains the engine of a US Army truck in the maintenance workshop at Camp Diane, base of the Civil Affairs team.

Bottom.
A young Bosnian Muslim and his mother walking in Kladanj behind an American soldier.

people walking around, more people getting out and I think that's a good blessing.

My view is that if America does stay here it should rotate every six months, not a whole year because it puts real stress on the soldiers, especially those who haven't been deployed before and don't really know what the Army's about. I've been in for four and a half years now and I know a lot about the military. I hope it doesn't break out into another war if we leave.

I miss my family. I have a two year old son and I ain't ever seen him grow up yet. Each individual in IFOR is supposed to get two weeks R&R in a year, to see their families, but it's tough on a lot of people. This problem will make a lot of people leave the military. Most of those who come to the military come for the education; basically they're not really here for the adventure which is what the Army here is all about.

Like any job in the world, it's good for some people and not so good for others. It's been a good learning experience

> **A lot of the people I wave at wave back but a lot of the others just throw their hands down, won't even wave. I'm doing this to help them but they just don't appreciate it. I guess that's just the attitude some people have.**

for myself. Hopefully, when I get out, I'll get a nice job. I wouldn't mind becoming like my brother, a police officer. Taking care of the family, that's the hardest thing for me – missing my family; I've just been married a year, the family hasn't really grown together.

Bosnia is a very beautiful country, it's an old style living like back in the days of the 1950s with horses and wagons, not really up to date. Some people are trying to make a change for the country but some people are just holding back. A lot of the people I wave at wave back but a lot of the others just throw their hands down, won't even wave. I'm doing this to help them but they just don't appreciate it. I guess that's just the attitude some people have.

In Haiti you could go into the town and talk to the people, see what was going on. Here, I guess because of the mines and that they haven't really come to an agreement, you can't do that. In Haiti the government was really taking over but here you have a conflict between religions and you just don't know who might be a sniper. It's basically just looking out for the welfare of the soldiers.

The United States Army is based on a concept of discipline, leading an example for other soldiers. Going out and getting drunk and partying – that's not our reason for being here. Our basic reason is to keep the peace and I think that's what the higher officers of the force are looking at.

Being inside the compound and drinking a beer or two to relieve the pressure, a Budweiser or a swig of beer, wouldn't hurt anybody. I'm not saying we're alcoholics but a beer would calm your nerves down, like on a Friday with the barbecue. In America you cannot go downtown or into a public restaurant and hold a beer or you would be arrested. You can't drink or drive, you can't do nothing. In Europe everybody's got a beer in his hand, in America you just can't do that or you would get a ticket.

This is just military discipline, the military leads the way. I guess that's why a lot of countries look up to America because they see the US Army, a well disciplined force, ready. They won't have any problem backing up other countries if they're having problems and need the help. Over the past years we've been in a lot of situations: Somalia, Haiti, Cuba and now Bosnia. You never know what's going to be next, it might be Lebanon or Korea or wherever. A lot of people ain't going to take no chance, they're going to want to get out and get more family time."

Top.
2nd Brigade Civil Affairs team going into a primary school in Kladanj with the aim of distributing pencils that were donated by a primary school in the USA.

Bottom.
A Bosnian Muslim in Kladanj points to indicted war criminal Radovan Karadzic in the IFOR newspaper **The Herald of Peace,** a free newspaper in Serbo Croatian that is distributed by Psy-Ops personnel throughout the IFOR divisions.

# Sergiu Olivia

PRIVATE, US ARMY, 4-12 INFANTRY, 2ND BRIGADE

### Interviewed on guard duty at Camp Diane

"This is my third deployment; I've been to Kuwait, Somalia and now here. I've been away for the last three years so basically I'm kind of used to this environment already. This is a little different from Somalia because you can see the effects taking place as you go out in convoy here. We would see how much destruction was done around this place and now you see kids playing on the streets, people building. To me it makes it all worthwhile.

It gets a little monotonous after a while but I still see the effect we're having and I think we're doing something good by being over here, I feel good. Not that I like being here, I don't like being here but I like the effect of us being here and that makes me feel good. The life's getting better, there's less incidents."

# David Scott MacDonald

LIEUTENANT, COMMANDER OF CAMP DIANE

### Interviewed in maintenance workshop, Camp Diane

"When we received our march orders to come down here the Battalion Commander called me into his office and said, 'Hey, I've heard you're doing a great job, so we want you to be the battalion's Maintenance Officer'. I said, 'I don't know anything about this maintenance stuff, I think you've got the wrong guy.' So, he said, 'Well, that's good, that way you'll learn good from Chief Black', and I was too in shock to argue with him. A month later we were deployed here.

At first, I think I was probably the greatest asshole that ever walked this earth. Anything and all, the smallest detail that I saw, was wrong. I would jump on it, chew somebody out, give somebody a hard time and I just rode people, probably more than I would have in hindsight. I chilled out a little bit. I think I relaxed quite a bit since I've been back from my R&R leave, saw my wife, saw my friends. When I was gone nothing fell apart, things were smooth when I got back. Now I have less to do because projects I had wanted done were done when I was gone.

The American Army is not really set up mentally to do this kind of mission. As a throwback to the Vietnam War we are so opposed to long deployments, long operations. What Americans like to do is get in, get the job done as fast as possible, as ruthlessly as possible, clean it all up and be done. To do a year project is really hard for us.

Probably the hardest thing we're having is that we're confined to our camps, so many restrictions. It's really frustrating, it's really surprising we don't have as many morale problems as we might. I'm surprised that soldiers aren't shooting each other, they haven't shot me yet, I'm surprised that they're not burning tyres and acting like people in a penitentiary. I think the reason for the restrictions is that everyone's afraid of blowing the good name of the American Army and the United States.

I think Europeans see a greater significance to a peace in the Balkans than Americans can. We're from the new world, it's kind of isolationist but, so what, if Bosnia gets out of hand, who cares, let them fight it out and win. I think Europeans see it more clearly as a

trouble spot; it's right on their doorstep, on their back door and it's a little more important.

America can throw in a lot of things that some countries can't. We can sustain an operation anywhere in the world for a long, long time. We can put in immense military and economic power, and even diplomatic influence, over a lot of different things – and maybe that's why people call for us to be involved. We want so many things from NATO that NATO expects us to chip in our fair share, which I think we are.

I don't know if it's going to succeed or not. I'm not sure when we leave that things will go on as they are now; working towards rebuilding the country, holding elections and getting people to where they are kind of free. What concerns us is that, when we leave at the end of the year, everything will come to nothing and they will start fighting again. That's hard for us.

But one thing is that you can see the kids playing and people rebuilding their stuff – right across the street. The guys come in here and re-roof their warehouse, they wouldn't be doing that if we weren't here. Maybe it gives them a little hope and a chance to take a break and rethink and maybe not want to go back to war. We'll have to see."

> What concerns us is that, when we leave at the end of the year, everything will come to nothing and they will start fighting again.

# IFOR on IFOR

First published in 1996 by
CONNECT
17 Jeffrey Street,
Edinburgh EH1 1DR
Scotland

ISBN 1 901205 00 2

Book design by Mark Blackadder

Printed in the
Republic of Slovenia by
Gorenjski Tisk, Kranj
on Nordland 135 gsm art paper
supplied by Europapier, Slovenia